14.95

BIOLOGICAL
AND CHEMICAL
WEAPONS

Other Books in the At Issue Series:

BIOLOGICAL AND CHEMICAL WEAPONS

David M. Haugen, *Book Editor*

David L. Bender, *Publisher*
Bruno Leone, *Executive Editor*
Bonnie Szumski, *Editorial Director*
Stuart B. Miller, *Managing Editor*

An Opposing Viewpoints® Series

Greenhaven Press, Inc.
San Diego, California

Library of Congress Cataloging-in-Publication Data

Biological and chemical weapons / David M. Haugen, book editor.
     p.   cm. — (At issue)
   Includes bibliographical references and index.
   ISBN 0-7377-0555-8 (pbk. : alk. paper) —
ISBN 0-7377-0556-6 (lib. bdg. : alk. paper)
    1. Biological warfare. 2. Chemical warfare. I. Haugen, David,
1969– . II. At issue (San Diego, Calif.)

UG447.8 .B53   2001
358'.3—dc21   00-030906
                                                 CIP

Table of Contents

Introduction

In 1998 police nationwide received reports from abortion clinics concerning mysterious envelopes that had arrived in the mail. Clinic personnel notified authorities immediately when they found that the envelopes contained stained pieces of paper bearing the message: "Anthrax. Have a nice death." Though terrified at first, the recipients of the envelopes calmed when lab tests determined the letters showed no trace of anthrax, a virulent disease that plagues livestock and can be equally fatal to humans. Authorities and clinic employees were convinced of a mass hoax, but subsequent sightings of these envelopes still prompted emergency phone calls. No one wanted to be the first victim of a "real" terrorist act. Hazardous material (hazmat) teams responded to every call, costing cities huge sums of money to address what was widely considered to be an empty threat.

The new threat

Journalists T. Trent Gegax and Mark Hosenball, in their *Newsweek* article, "The New Bomb Threat," maintain, "The specter of bioterrorism forces law-enforcement officials to take such nonsense very seriously." Bioterrorism is the popularized term for terrorist attacks using weapons of a biological nature, typically disease-causing pathogens that can spread easily throughout a concentrated population. The desire of perpetrators may be to disable the victims or kill them outright. The fear associated with these types of weapons is that a large population can be infected by doses small enough (a few spores, perhaps) that they could be easily concealed. Furthermore, many people believe that since the germs are common, they could be obtained or even grown with little technical expertise or equipment. Some experts, however, disagree. Gegax and Hosenball note that "Though anthrax is deadly, it isn't easy to transform the spores into a usable weapon." Still, the possibility exists, and the public, its fears fueled in part by popular novels that portray the horrifying potential of such terrorist acts, feels vulnerable.

The fear, of course, is not only a byproduct of science fiction scenarios. In 1995 the Aum Shinrikyo cult in Japan released sarin nerve gas in a Tokyo subway, killing twelve people and contaminating thousands more. Like biological agents, sarin gas is relatively easy to manufacture and conceal, making it an ideal weapon for terrorists. The nerve gas was carried on board the subway in plastic bags. With the possibility that chemical or biological weapons could be transported or delivered anywhere, the fear of vulnerability may be justified.

Coupled with the fear of clandestine manufacture and movement of chemical or biological agents is a growing apprehension of terrorists' enigmatic motivations. Traditionally, terrorist groups shun mass killings because the backlash may cast a negative light on their political cause. But many of today's terrorist groups like the Aum Shinrikyo may be acting without a political agenda. The Aum Shinrikyo, for example, were religious fanatics apparently acting out part of a larger doomsday plot; other groups may simply want the celebrity of media attention that results from such attacks. As Ron Purver, a strategic analyst for the Canadian Security Intelligence Service, argues, "What makes these groups especially dangerous is that they may not be constrained by some of the political disincentives—fear of alienating potential supporters or of unleashing massive government retribution, etc.—that may have operated in the past in the case of more traditional terrorist groups."

Exaggerated fears?

Once the sarin gas attack was public knowledge, some officials predicted that the floodgates had been opened and that other copycat attacks would take place. No such attacks have yet materialized, however. And analysts who believe the fear of chemical and biological terrorist attacks is exaggerated point out that few attacks involving these weapons have ever been attempted and, of the significant attempts, most have been thwarted by authorities. In fact, the most infamous terrorist attack in recent decades was the bombing of the Murrah Federal Building in Oklahoma City and that involved a traditional explosive device. Marie Isabelle Chevrier, a member of the Federation of American Scientists Working Group on Biological and Toxin Weapons Verification, asserts the "hopeful" prophecy that the Oklahoma City bombing "demonstrates how effective, and visually riveting, relatively simple explosive devices can be. Perhaps one of the unintended but nevertheless welcome consequences of that bombing is that terrorists need not turn to C/B [chemical/biological] weapons to command the public's undivided attention or to produce high casualties."

The irony of Chevrier's conclusion is certainly not humorous. Those who refute the doomsayers argue that the reasons for not using chemical and biological weapons are so strong that most terrorist groups would refrain. To these individuals, the disincentives that Ron Purver calls outdated—fear of alienating supporters or attracting government retribution—are in fact still holding terrorist groups in check. Moreover, evidence shows that the groups who have tried to implement chemical or biological agents have either failed to carry out the threat or—in the case of the successful poisonings—failed to produce mass death.

The fear, however, remains. The deadly potential of a nuclear device carried in a rocket payload has been shrunk to a biological weapon that some alarmists claim could fit in a pocket. In the case of a biological or chemical attack, no radar or early warning device could foretell of the coming doom, and it is that unpredictability that worries government officials and ordinary citizens alike. Millions of dollars are now funding measures to deter, detect, and respond to chemical and biological weapons threats in the United States. Both sides of the bioterrorism debate are forced to concede that only time will tell if it is money well spent.

1

Biological Weapons Are a Serious Threat

Richard K. Betts

Richard K. Betts is the Director of National Security Studies at the Council on Foreign Relations, and he is a professor of political science and Director of the Institute for War and Peace Studies at Columbia University.

Although the potential for nuclear annihilation has been reduced with the end of the Cold War, America still faces attacks by weapons of mass destruction. Since the United States now has a military edge over its old enemies, the concern for nuclear deterrence should take a back seat to providing protection against small terrorist attacks involving biological weapons. Biological weapons have a catastrophic killing potential and they are easy to make and conceal. American defensive measures, however, still labor under the assumed threats of the Cold War era and are inadequate in dealing with attacks involving biological agents. If the United States is determined to remain strong in a world where biological weapons are a viable option to domestic and foreign terrorists, then the government will have to rethink both its strategies concerning civil defense and its role in foreign affairs.

During the Cold War, weapons of mass destruction were the centerpiece of foreign policy. Nuclear arms hovered in the background of every major issue in East-West competition and alliance relations. The highest priorities of U.S. policy could almost all be linked in some way to the danger of World War III and the fear of millions of casualties in the American homeland.

Since the Cold War, other matters have displaced strategic concerns on the foreign policy agenda, and that agenda itself is now barely on the public's radar screen. Apart from defense policy professionals, few Americans still lose sleep over weapons of mass destruction (WMD). After all, what do normal people feel is the main relief provided by the end of the Cold War? It is that the danger of nuclear war is off their backs.

Reprinted from "The New Threat of Mass Destruction," by Richard K. Betts, *Foreign Affairs,* January/February 1998, vol. 77, no. 1. Copyright ©1998 by the Council on Foreign Relations, Inc. Reprinted by permission of *Foreign Affairs.*

New worries

Yet today, WMD present more and different things to worry about than during the Cold War. For one, nuclear arms are no longer the only concern, as chemical and biological weapons have come to the fore. For another, there is less danger of complete annihilation, but more danger of mass destruction. Since the Cold War is over and American and Russian nuclear inventories are much smaller, there is less chance of an apocalyptic exchange of many thousands of weapons. But the probability that some smaller number of WMD will be used is growing. Many of the standard strategies and ideas for coping with WMD threats are no longer as relevant as they were when Moscow was the main adversary. But new thinking has not yet congealed in as clear a form as the Cold War concepts of nuclear deterrence theory.

The new dangers have not been ignored inside the Beltway. "Counterproliferation" has become a cottage industry in the Pentagon and the intelligence community, and many worthwhile initiatives to cope with threats are under way. Some of the most important implications of the new era, however, have not yet registered on the public agenda. This in turn limits the inclination of politicians to push some appropriate programs. Even the defense establishment has directed its attention mainly toward countering threats WMD pose to U.S. military forces operating abroad rather than to the more worrisome danger that mass destruction will occur in the United States, killing large numbers of civilians.

The points to keep in mind about the new world of mass destruction are the following. First, the roles such weapons play in international conflict are changing. They no longer represent the technological frontier of warfare. Increasingly, they will be weapons of the weak-states or groups that militarily are at best second-class. The importance of the different types among them has also shifted. Biological weapons should now be the most serious concern, with nuclear weapons second and chemicals a distant third.

Today . . . there is less danger of complete annihilation, but more danger of mass destruction.

Second, the mainstays of Cold War security policy—deterrence and arms control—are not what they used to be. Some new threats may not be deterrable, and the role of arms control in dealing with WMD has been marginalized. In a few instances, continuing devotion to deterrence and arms control may have side effects that offset the benefits.

Third, some of the responses most likely to cope with the threats in novel ways will not find a warm welcome. The response that should now be the highest priority is one long ignored, opposed, or ridiculed: a serious civil defense program to blunt the effects of WMD if they are unleashed within the United States. Some of the most effective measures to prevent attacks within the United States may also challenge traditional civil liberties if pursued to the maximum. And the most troubling conclusion for foreign policy as a whole is that reducing the odds of attacks in the United States might require pulling back from involvement in some foreign conflicts. American activism to guarantee international stability is, paradoxically, the prime source of American vulnerability.

This was partly true in the Cold War, when the main danger that nuclear weapons might detonate on U.S. soil sprang from strategic engagement in Europe, Asia, and the Middle East to deter attacks on U.S. allies. But engagement then assumed a direct link between regional stability and U.S. survival. The connection is less evident today, when there is no globally threatening superpower or transnational ideology to be contained—only an array of serious but entirely local disruptions. Today, as the only nation acting to police areas outside its own region, the United States makes itself a target for states or groups whose aspirations are frustrated by U.S. power.

From modern to primitive

When nuclear weapons were born, they represented the most advanced military applications of science, technology, and engineering. None but the great powers could hope to obtain them. By now, however, nuclear arms have been around for more than half a century, and chemical and biological weapons even longer. They are not just getting old. In the strategic terms most relevant to American security, they have become primitive. Once the military cutting edge of the strong, they have become the only hope for so-called rogue states or terrorists who want to contest American power. Why? Because the United States has developed overwhelming superiority in conventional military force—something it never thought it had against the Soviet Union.

The Persian Gulf War of 1991 demonstrated the American advantage in a manner that stunned many abroad. Although the U.S. defense budget has plunged, other countries are not closing the gap. U.S. military spending remains more than triple that of any potentially hostile power and higher than the combined defense budgets of Russia, China, Iran, Iraq, North Korea, and Cuba.

More to the point, there is no evidence that those countries' level of military professionalism is rising at a rate that would make them competitive even if they were to spend far more on their forces. Rolling along in what some see as a revolution in military affairs, American forces continue to make unmatched use of state-of-the-art weapons, surveillance and information systems, and the organizational and doctrinal flexibility for managing the integration of these complex innovations into "systems of systems" that is the key to modern military effectiveness. More than ever in military history, brains are brawn. Even if hostile countries somehow catch up in an arms race, their military organizations and cultures are unlikely to catch up in the competence race for management, technology assimilation, and combat command skills.

If it is infeasible for hostile states to counter the United States in conventional combat, it is even more daunting for smaller groups such as terrorists. If the United States is lucky, the various violent groups with grievances against the American government and society will continue to think up schemes using conventional explosives. Few terrorist groups have shown an interest in inflicting true mass destruction. Bombings or hostage seizures have generally threatened no more than a few hundred lives. Let us hope that this limitation has been due to a powerful underlying reason, rather than a simple lack of capability, and that the few exceptions do not become more typical.

If the United States is lucky, the various violent groups with grievances against the American government and society will continue to think up schemes using conventional explosives.

There is no sure reason to bet on such restraint. Indeed, some have tried to use WMD, only to see them fizzle. The Japanese Aum Shinrikyo cult released sarin nerve gas in Tokyo in 1995 but killed only a few people, and some analysts believe that those who attacked the World Trade Center in 1993 laced their bomb with cyanide, which burned up in the explosion (this was not confirmed, but a large amount of cyanide was found in the perpetrators' possession). Eventually such a group will prove less incompetent. If terrorists decide that they want to stun American policymakers by inflicting enormous damage, WMD become more attractive at the same time that they are becoming more accessible.

Finally, unchallenged military superiority has shifted the attention of the U.S. military establishment away from WMD. During the Cold War, nuclear weapons were the bedrock of American war capabilities. They were the linchpin of defense debate, procurement programs, and arms control because the United States faced another superpower—one that conventional wisdom feared could best it in conventional warfare. Today, no one cares about the MX missile or B-1 bomber, and hardly anyone really cares about the Strategic Arms Reduction Treaty. In a manner that could only have seemed ludicrous during the Cold War, proponents now rationalize the $2 billion B-2 as a weapon for conventional war. Hardly anyone in the Pentagon is still interested in how the United States could use WMD for its own strategic purposes.

What military planners are interested in is how to keep adversaries from using WMD as an "asymmetric" means to counter U.S. conventional power, and how to protect U.S. ground and naval forces abroad from WMD attacks. This concern is all well and good, but it abets a drift of attention away from the main danger. The primary risk is not that enemies might lob some nuclear or chemical weapons at U.S. armored battalions or ships, awful as that would be. Rather, it is that they might attempt to punish the United States by triggering catastrophes in American cities.

Emphasis on chemical weapons is wrongheaded

Until the past decade, the issue was nuclear arms, period. Chemical weapons received some attention from specialists, but never made the priority list of presidents and cabinets. Biological weapons were almost forgotten after they were banned by the 1972 Biological Weapons Convention. Chemical and biological arms have received more attention in the 1990s. The issues posed by the trio lumped under the umbrella of mass destruction differ, however. Most significantly, biological weapons have received less attention than the others but probably represent the greatest danger.

Chemical weapons have been noticed more in the past decade, especially since they were used by Iraq against Iranian troops in the 1980–88 Iran-Iraq War and against Kurdish civilians in 1988. Chemicals are far more widely available than nuclear weapons because the technology required to produce them is far simpler, and large numbers of countries have undertaken chemical weapons programs. But chemical weapons are not really in the same class as other weapons of mass destruction, in the sense of ability to inflict a huge number of civilian casualties in a single strike. For the tens of thousands of fatalities as in, say, the biggest strategic bombing raids of World War II, it would be very difficult logistically and operationally to deliver chemical weapons in necessary quantities over wide areas.

Nevertheless, much attention and effort have been lavished on a campaign to eradicate chemical weapons. This may be a good thing, but the side effects are not entirely benign. For one, banning chemicals means that for deterrence, nuclear weapons become even more important than they used to be. That is because a treaty cannot assuredly prevent hostile nations from deploying chemical weapons, while the United States has forsworn the option to retaliate in kind.

Biological weapons have received less attention than [other weapons of mass destruction] but probably represent the greatest danger.

In the past, the United States had a no-first-use policy for chemical weapons but reserved the right to strike back with them if an enemy used them first. The 1993 Chemical Weapons Convention (CWC), which entered into force last April [1997], requires the United States to destroy its stockpile, thus ending this option. The United States did the same with biological arms long ago, during the Nixon administration. Eliminating its own chemical and biological weapons practically precludes a no-first-use policy for nuclear weapons, since they become the only WMD available for retaliation.

Would the United States follow through and use nuclear weapons against a country or group that had killed several thousand Americans with deadly chemicals? It is hard to imagine breaking the post-Nagasaki taboo in that situation. But schemes for conventional military retaliation would not suffice without detracting from the force of American deterrent threats. There would be a risk for the United States in setting a precedent that someone could use WMD against Americans without suffering similar destruction in return. Limiting the range of deterrent alternatives available to U.S. strategy will not necessarily cause deterrence to fail, but it will certainly not strengthen it.

The ostensible benefit of the CWC is that it will make chemical arms harder to acquire and every bit as illegal and stigmatized as biological weapons have been for a quarter-century. If it has that benefit, what effect will the ban have on the choices of countries or groups who want some kind of WMD in any case, whether for purposes of deterrence, aggression, or revenge? At the margin, the ban will reduce the disincentives to acquiring biological weapons, since they will be no less illegal, no harder to obtain or conceal, and far more damaging than chemical weapons. If major reductions in the chemical threat produce even minor increases in the biological threat, it will be a bad trade.

If major reductions in the chemical threat produce even minor increases in the biological threat, it will be a bad trade.

One simple fact should worry Americans more about biological than about nuclear or chemical arms: unlike either of the other two, biological weapons combine maximum destructiveness and easy availability. Nuclear arms have great killing capacity but are hard to get; chemical weapons are easy to get but lack such killing capacity; biological agents have both qualities. A 1993 study by the Office of Technology Assessment concluded that a single airplane delivering 100 kilograms of anthrax spores—a dormant phase of a bacillus that multiplies rapidly in the body, producing toxins and rapid hemorrhaging—by aerosol on a clear, calm night over the Washington, D.C., area could kill between one million and three million people, 300 times as many fatalities as if the plane had delivered sarin gas in amounts ten times larger.

Like chemical weapons but unlike nuclear weapons, biologicals are relatively easy to make. Innovations in biotechnology have obviated many of the old problems in handling and preserving biological agents, and many have been freely available for scientific research. Nuclear weapons are not likely to be the WMD of choice for non-state terrorist groups. They require huge investments and targetable infrastructure, and are subject to credible threats by the United States. An aggrieved group that decides it wants to kill huge numbers of Americans will find the mission easier to accomplish with anthrax than with a nuclear explosion.

Inside the Pentagon, concern about biological weapons has picked up tremendously in the past couple of years, but there is little serious attention to the problem elsewhere. This could be a good thing if nothing much can be done, since publicity might only give enemies ideas. But it is a bad thing if it impedes efforts to take steps—such as civil defense—that could blunt nuclear, chemical, or biological attacks.

Deterrence and arms control in decline

An old vocabulary still dominates policy discussion of WMD. Rhetoric in the defense establishment falls back on the all-purpose strategic buzzword of the Cold War: deterrence. But deterrence now covers fewer of the threats the United States faces than it did during the Cold War.

The logic of deterrence is clearest when the issue is preventing unprovoked and unambiguous aggression, when the aggressor recognizes that it is the aggressor rather than the defender. Deterrence is less reliable when both sides in a conflict see each other as the aggressor. When the United States intervenes in messy Third World conflicts, the latter is often true. In such cases, the side that the United States wants to deter may see itself as trying to deter the United States. Such situations are ripe for miscalculation.

For the country that used to be the object of U.S. deterrence—Russia—the strategic burden has been reversed. Based on assumptions of Soviet conventional military superiority, U.S. strategy used to rely on the threat to escalate—to be the first to use nuclear weapons during a war—to deter attack by Soviet armored divisions. Today the tables have turned. There is no Warsaw Pact, Russia has half or less of the military potential of the Soviet Union, and its current conventional forces are in disarray, while NATO is expanding eastward. It is now Moscow that has the incentive to compensate for conventional weakness by placing heavier reliance on nuclear capabilities. The Russians adopted a nuclear no-first-use policy in the early 1980s, but renounced it after their precipitous post–Cold War decline.

Today Russia needs to be reassured, not deterred. The main danger from Russian WMD is leakage from vast stockpiles to anti-American groups elsewhere—the "loose nukes" problem. So long as the United States has no intention of attacking the Russians, their greater reliance on nuclear forces is not a problem. If the United States has an interest in reducing nuclear stockpiles, however, it is. The traditional American approach—thinking in terms of its own deterrence strategies—provides no guidance. Indeed, noises some Americans still make about deterring the Russians compound the problem by reinforcing Moscow's alarm.

The main danger from Russian WMD is leakage from vast stockpiles to anti-American groups elsewhere.

Similarly, U.S. conventional military superiority gives China an incentive to consider more reliance on an escalation strategy. The Chinese have a long-standing no-first-use policy but adopted it when their strategic doctrine was that of "people's war," which relied on mass mobilization and low-tech weaponry. Faith in that doctrine was severely shaken by the American performance in the Persian Gulf War. Again, the United States might assume that there is no problem as long as Beijing only wants to deter and the United States does not want to attack. But how do these assumptions relate to the prospect of a war over Taiwan? That is a conflict that no one wants but that can hardly be ruled out in light of evolving tensions. If the United States decides openly to deter Beijing from attacking Taiwan, the old lore from the Cold War may be relevant. But if Washington continues to leave policy ambiguous, who will know who is deterring whom? Ambiguity is a recipe for confusion and miscalculation in a time of crisis. For all the upsurge of attention in the national security establishment to the prospect of conflict with China, there has been remarkably little discussion of the role of nuclear weapons in a Sino-American collision.

The main problem for deterrence, however, is that it still relies on the corpus of theory that undergirded Cold War policy, dominated by reliance on the threat of second-strike retaliation. But retaliation requires knowledge of who has launched an attack and the address at which they reside. These requirements are not a problem when the threat comes from a government, but they are if the enemy is anonymous. Today some groups may wish to punish the United States without taking credit for the action—a mass killing equivalent to the 1988 bombing of Pan Am Flight 103 over Lockerbie, Scotland. Moreover, the options the defense establishment favors have shifted over entirely from deterrence to preemption. The majority of those who dealt with nuclear weapons policy during the Cold War adamantly opposed developing first-strike options. Today, scarcely anyone looks to that old logic when thinking about rogues or terrorists, and most hope to be able to mount a disarming action against any group with WMD.

Overall . . . the problem with arms control is not that it does too much but that it now does relatively little.

Finally, eliminating chemical weapons trims some options for deterrence. Arms control restrictions on the instruments that can be used for deterrent threats are not necessarily the wrong policy, but they do work against maximizing deterrence. Overall, however, the problem with arms control is not that it does too much but that it now does relatively little.

From the Limited Test Ban negotiations in the 1960s through the Strategic Arms Limitation Talks, Strategic Arms Reduction [Treaty], and Intermediate-range Nuclear Forces negotiations in the 1970s and 1980s, arms control treaties were central to managing WMD threats. Debates about whether particular agreements with Moscow were in the United States' interest were bitter because everyone believed that the results mattered. Today there is no consensus that treaties regulating armaments matter much. Among national security experts, the corps that pays close attention to START and Conventional Forces in Europe negotiations has shrunk. With the exception of the Chemical Weapons Convention, efforts to control WMD by treaty have become small potatoes. The biggest recent news in arms control has not been any negotiation to regulate WMD, but a campaign to ban land mines.

The United States' Cold War partner in arms control, Russia, has disarmed a great deal voluntarily. But despite standard rhetoric, the United States has not placed a high priority on convincing Moscow to divest itself of more of its nuclear weapons; the Clinton administration has chosen to promote NATO expansion, which pushes the Russians in the opposite direction.

The 1968 Nuclear Nonproliferation Treaty [NPT] remains a hallowed institution, but it has nowhere new to go. It will not convert the problem countries that want to obtain WMD—unless, like Iraq and North Korea in the 1980s, they sign and accept the legal obligation and then simply cheat. The NPT regime will continue to impede access to fissile materials on the open market, but it will not do so in novel or more effective ways. And it does not address the problem of Russian "loose nukes" any better than the Russian and American governments do on their own.

Civil defense

Despite all the new limitations, deterrence remains an important aspect of strategy. There is not much the United States needs to do to keep up its deterrence capability, however, given the thousands of nuclear weapons and the conventional military superiority it has. Where capabilities are grossly underdeveloped, however, is the area of responses for coping should deterrence fail.

Enthusiasts for defensive capability, mostly proponents of the Strategic Defense Initiative [SDI] from the Reagan years, remain fixated on the least relevant form of it: high-tech active defenses to intercept ballistic missiles. There is still scant interest in what should now be the first priority: civil defense preparations to cope with uses of WMD within the United States. Active defenses against missiles would be expensive investments that might or might not work against a threat the United States probably will not face for years, but would do nothing against the threat it already faces. Civil defense measures are extremely cheap and could prove far more effective than they would have against a large-scale Soviet attack.

During the Cold War, debate about antimissile defense concerned whether it was technologically feasible or cost-effective and whether it would threaten the Soviets and ignite a spiraling arms race between offensive and defensive weapons. One need not refight the battles over SDI to see that the relevance to current WMD threats is tenuous. Iraq, Iran, or North Korea will not be able to deploy intercontinental missiles for years. Nor, if they are strategically cunning, should they want to. For the limited number of nuclear warheads these countries are likely to have, and especially for biological weapons, other means of delivery are more easily available. Alternatives to ballistic missiles include aircraft, ship-launched cruise missiles, and unconventional means, such as smuggling, at which the intelligence agencies of these countries have excelled. Non-state perpetrators like those who bombed the World Trade Center will choose clandestine means of necessity.

If a larger part of the worry about WMD these days is about their use by terrorist states or groups, the odds are higher that sometime, somewhere in the country, some of these weapons will go off, despite the best efforts to stop them.

A ballistic missile defense system, whether it costs more or less than the $60 billion the Congressional Budget Office recently estimated would be required for one limited option, will not counter these modes of attack. Indeed, if a larger part of the worry about WMD these days is about their use by terrorist states or groups, the odds are higher that sometime, somewhere in the country, some of these weapons will go off, despite the best efforts to stop them. If that happens, the United States should have in place whatever measures can mitigate the consequences.

By the later phases of the Cold War it was hard to get people interested in civil defense against an all-out Soviet attack that could detonate thousands of high-yield nuclear weapons in U.S. population centers. To many, the lives that would have been saved seemed less salient than the many millions that would still have been lost. It should be easier to see the value of civil defense, however, in the context of more limited attacks, perhaps with only a few low-yield weapons. A host of minor measures can increase protection or recovery from biological, nuclear, or chemical effects. Examples are stockpiling or distribution of protective masks; equipment and training for decontamination; standby programs for mass vaccinations and emergency treatment with antibiotics; wider and deeper planning of emergency response procedures; and public education about hasty sheltering and emergency actions to reduce individual vulnerability.

Both then and now, there has been a powerful reason that civil defense efforts have been unpopular: they alarm people. They remind them that their vulnerability to mass destruction is not a bad dream.

Such programs would not make absorbing a WMD attack tolerable. But inadequacy is no excuse for neglecting actions that could reduce death and suffering, even if the difference in casualties is small. Civil defenses are especially worthwhile considering that they are extraordinarily cheap compared with regular military programs or active defense systems. Yet until recently, only half a billion dollars—less than two-tenths of one percent of the defense budget and less than $2 a head for every American—went to chemical and biological defense, while nearly $4 billion was spent annually on ballistic missile defense. Why haven't policymakers attended to first things first—cheap programs that can cushion the effects of a disaster—before undertaking expensive programs that provide no assurance they will be able to prevent it?

One problem is conceptual inertia. The Cold War accustomed strategists to worrying about an enemy with thousands of WMD, rather than foes with a handful. For decades the question of strategic defense was also posed as a debate between those who saw no alternative to relying on deterrence and those who hoped that an astrodome over the United States could replace deterrence with invulnerability. None of these hoary fixations address the most probable WMD threats in the post–Cold War world.

Opposition to Cold War civil defense programs underlies psychological aversion to them now. Opponents used to argue that civil defense was a dangerous illusion because it could do nothing significant to reduce the horror of an attack that would obliterate hundreds of cities, because it would promote a false sense of security, and because it could even be destabilizing and provoke attack in a crisis. Whether or not such arguments were valid then, they are not now. But both then and now, there has been a powerful reason that civil defense efforts have been unpopular: they alarm people. They remind them that their vulnerability to mass destruction is not a bad dream, not something that strategic schemes for deterrence, preemption, or interception are sure to solve.

Playing Globocop feeds the urge of aggrieved groups to strike back.

Civil defense can limit damage but not minimize it. For example, some opponents may be able to develop biological agents that circumvent available vaccines and antibiotics. (Those with marginal technical capabilities, however, might be stopped by blocking the easier options.) Which is worse—the limitations of defenses, or having to answer for failure to try? The moment that WMD are used somewhere in a manner that produces tens of thousands of fatalities, there will be hysterical outbursts of all sorts. One of them will surely be, "Why didn't the government prepare us for this?" It is not in the long-term interest of political leaders to indulge popular aversion. If public resistance under current circumstances prevents widespread distribution, stockpiling, and instruction in the use of defensive equipment or medical services, the least that should be done is to optimize plans and preparations to rapidly implement such activities when the first crisis ignites demand.

As threats of terrorism using WMD are taken more seriously, interest will grow in preemptive defense measures—the most obvious of which is intensified intelligence collection. Where this involves targeting groups within the United States that might seem to be potential breeding grounds for terrorists (for example, supporters of Palestinian militants, home-grown militias or cults, or radicals with ties to Iran, Iraq, or Libya), controversies will arise over constitutional limits on invasion of privacy or search and seizure. So long as the WMD danger remains hypothetical, such controversies will not be easily resolved. They have not come to the fore so far because U.S. law enforcement has been unbelievably lucky in apprehending terrorists. The group arrested in 1993 for planning to bomb the Lincoln Tunnel happened to be infiltrated by an informer, and Timothy McVeigh happened to be picked up in 1995 for driving without a license plate. Those who fear compromising civil liberties with permissive standards for government snooping should consider what is likely to happen once such luck runs out and it proves impossible to identify perpetrators. Suppose a secretive radical Islamic group launches a biological attack, kills 100,000 people, and announces that it will do the same thing again if its terms are not met. (The probability of such a scenario may not be high, but it can no longer be consigned to science fiction.) In that case, it is hardly unthinkable that a panicked legal system would roll over and treat Arab-Americans as it did the Japanese-Americans who were herded into concentration camps after Pearl Harbor. Stretching limits on domestic surveillance to reduce the chances of facing such choices could be the lesser evil.

Is isolationism the best defense?

No programs aimed at controlling adversaries' capabilities can eliminate the dangers. One risk is that in the more fluid politics of the post–Cold War world, the United States could stumble into an unanticipated crisis with Russia or China. There are no well-established rules of the game to brake a spiraling conflict over the Baltic states or Taiwan, as there were in the superpower competition after the Cuban missile crisis. The second danger is that some angry group that blames the United States for its problems may decide to coerce Americans, or simply exact vengeance, by inflicting devastation on them where they live.

If steps to deal with the problem in terms of capabilities are limited, can anything be done to address intentions—the incentives of any foreign power or group to lash out at the United States? There are few answers to this question that do not compromise the fundamental strategic activism and internationalist thrust of U.S. foreign policy over the past half-century. That is because the best way to keep people from believing that the United States is responsible for their problems is to avoid involvement in their conflicts.

Ever since the Munich agreement [a failed attempt to limit Adolf Hitler's expansionist policy] and Pearl Harbor, with only a brief interruption during the decade after the Tet offensive [during Vietnam], there has been a consensus that if Americans did not draw their defense perimeter far forward and confront foreign troubles in their early stages, those troubles would come to them at home. But because the United States is now the only superpower and weapons of mass destruction have become more accessible, American intervention in troubled areas is not so much a way to fend off such threats as it is what stirs them up.

Will U.S. involvement in unstable situations around the former U.S.S.R. head off conflict with Moscow or generate it? Will making NATO bigger and moving it to Russia's doorstep deter Russian pressure on Ukraine and the Baltics or provoke it? With Russia and China, there is less chance that either will set out to conquer Europe or Asia than that they will try to restore old sovereignties and security zones by reincorporating new states of the former Soviet Union or the province of Taiwan. None of this means that NATO expansion or support for Taiwan's autonomy will cause nuclear war. It does mean that to whatever extent American activism increases those countries' incentives to rely on WMD while intensifying political friction between them and Washington, it is counterproductive.

The other main danger is the ire of smaller states or religious and cultural groups that see the United States as an evil force blocking their legitimate aspirations. It is hardly likely that Middle Eastern radicals would be hatching schemes like the destruction of the World Trade Center if the United States had not been identified for so long as the mainstay of Israel, the shah of Iran, and conservative Arab regimes and the source of a cultural assault on Islam. Cold War triumph magnified the problem. U.S. military and cultural hegemony—the basic threats to radicals seeking to challenge the status quo—are directly linked to the imputation of American responsibility for maintaining world order. Playing Globocop feeds the urge of aggrieved groups to strike back.

Is this a brief for isolationism? No. It is too late to turn off foreign resentments by retreating, even if that were an acceptable course. Alienated groups and governments would not stop blaming Washington for their problems. In addition, there is more to foreign policy than dampening incentives to hurt the United States. It is not automatically sensible to stop pursuing other interests for the sake of uncertain reductions in a threat of uncertain probability. Security is not all of a piece, and survival is only part of security.

But it is no longer prudent to assume that important security interests complement each other as they did during the Cold War. The interest at the very core—protecting the American homeland from attack—may now often be in conflict with security more broadly conceived and with the interests that mandate promoting American political values, economic interdependence, social Westernization, and stability in regions beyond Western Europe and the Americas. The United States should not give up all its broader political interests, but it should tread cautiously in areas—especially the Middle East—where broader interests grate against the core imperative of preventing mass destruction within America's borders.

2

Is the Fear of Biological Terrorism Justified?

Peter Pringle

Peter Pringle is a journalist who has worked for the London Sunday
Times *and the* Independent. *He is also the author of* Cornered: Big
Tobacco at the Bar of Justice, *an account of the major lawsuit settle-
ments against U.S. tobacco companies in 1997.*

Biological terrorist threats are multiplying even though few incidents of such terrorism have actually been carried out. The
threats, however, are being taken seriously, especially in the
United States where media fascination with new weapons of mass
destruction has fueled a growing fear for public safety. The fear,
however, is unjustified for two prominent reasons: the scenarios
described in such media hype are so fantastic that experts claim
they could not occur, and there is no precedent for any acts of
mass biological terrorism in the many decades in which these
weapons have been available. Indeed, the behavior of most terrorist groups is known to authorities, and any planned biological
attack would be identified well in advance of execution.

C ase one: on Christmas Eve last year [1998], 200 people were doing
their last-minute shopping at a department store in Palm Desert, California, when police surrounded the building and herded everyone into a
parking lot, ordering them to remove their clothes before hosing them
down with a bleach solution. An anonymous caller to 911 had claimed
that spores of the deadly anthrax bacteria had been released into the air
in the store. After carrying out tests, the police concluded that the call
was a hoax and the shoppers were allowed home. Two: on Boxing Day,
800 young people were partying at the Glass House Club, a dance hall in
Pomona, near Los Angeles, when police burst in. No one was allowed to
leave the building. Another 911 caller had warned of anthrax spores in
the air-conditioning system. For four hours the police searched for evidence of the bacteria. This call, too, was found to be a hoax. Three: a week
later, students and staff at a high school in Anaheim, California, were

Reprinted from "Infected by Fear," by Peter Pringle, *The Independent*, January 31, 1999. Reprinted
with permission from the author.

placed in quarantine for three hours while police dealt with another (false) anthrax alert. Four: on 14 January [1999], a public library in Oregon was closed after yet another. Five: two 14-year-old boys from Indiana were suspended from their school after plotting to send their teacher an envelope containing dried cinnamon, which they claimed in the accompanying note was anthrax spores. They had hatched the plan in an attempt to escape a test.

Rampant hoaxes

Anthrax has become a fad in America. The incidents described are not isolated: hoax calls about deadly biological agents—usually anthrax—are being made all over the country. Last year, there were about 50 anthrax hoaxes, and the rate is increasing. So far, only one suspect has been arrested. He is a 53-year-old accountant who was accused of trying to delay his appearance at a bankruptcy hearing by calling the courthouse and claiming that anthrax had been released into the air-conditioning system.

Threats such as these often result in the federal disaster teams known as HAZMATs (for hazardous materials) being sent running for their shiny protective suits and gas masks. The hoaxes are not only disruptive, they are extremely expensive. Testing the air and decontaminating buildings and people can cost as much as half a million dollars per hoax.

Police and public health officials claim to be so confounded by the hoaxes that they hark back to the good old days when the worst they had to deal with was a straightforward bomb scare. "Anthrax has really taken off nationwide," says an FBI spokesman, John Hoos. "We don't know why, but it's one of those sexy terms of the Nineties." Another FBI agent sighs, "I think we're dealing with nuts out there who are watching too much of *The X Files*." In fact, the origins of this epidemic, if it can be termed such, are easy to trace. If cranks and cultists are using anthrax as a terror hoax, it's because they've been told by the media that it's the greatest threat to American security since Soviet nuclear missiles. After the Gulf War in 1990, at which time most Americans probably thought it was a brand of bathroom cleaner, anthrax was blasted as the poor man's weapon of mass destruction. Alarmists have suggested that it would be ideal for use by mad cultists/international terrorists/rogue dictators (delete as appropriate). Beached by the end of the Cold War, planners in the Pentagon and military think-tanks sniffed around for potential new threats: in the annals of threat politics, international terrorism has an enduring ring to it. The media, too, cast about for bogeymen and found the former Soviet Union's rusting biological weapons labs and penniless scientists, whom it judged potential aiders and abetters to the new bioterrorists.

Easily transported; unpleasant symptoms leading to certain death; tiny quantities sufficient to wipe out entire cities: the sicko—or screenwriter—appeal of biological weapons was obvious. The public has been bombarded with horrific descriptions of what these agents do to you. Anthrax spores, found naturally in diseased sheep and cattle, can live for years in the soil, and can be transmitted on the wind or by skin contact. Victims develop a high fever and large sores before suffocating to death.

Such gruesome detail lends itself to fiction, and Americans have been treated to an onslaught of novels and television shows featuring futuristic biogenetically engineered microbes that have the potential to destroy all life on the planet. One example is *The Cobra Event,* a novel by Richard Preston about a germ attack on Manhattan involving a mixture of smallpox and cold viruses. Evidently, it was when President Clinton read this book that he started to push for the stockpiling of vaccines against germ weapons.

Each time Saddam Hussein (whose scientists, it has emerged, received at least one of their original sources of anthrax from an American biological repository in Maryland) refuses to allow UN inspectors to view his arsenal, anthrax is once again all over the news, and fears are fuelled. The politicians, too, have been doing their fair share of scaremongering: during one of the recent Iraq crises, Bill Cohen, the Secretary of Defense, appeared on television holding a bag of sugar and telling viewers that an equivalent amount of anthrax could kill half the population of Washington, D.C. Under the threat of another war with Iraq, all 2.4 million American troops are being vaccinated against anthrax. In addition, a whole vocabulary has now grown up around biological terrorism. Experts speak of "bioweapons", "biocriminals" and of our new, dangerous era of "postmodern terrorism". Anthrax in this lexicon is a WMD (Weapon of Mass Destruction), and according to U.S. government officials it's not a question of if it will be used, but when.

Taking the threat seriously

So, hoaxers aside, America is taking the threat very seriously. The nation is now spending $7 billion a year on defending itself against chemical, biological and nuclear terrorism. Any new government project to do with terrorism goes directly to the top of the pile in Congress. The Pentagon has ordered numerous devices for sniffing out nerve gases and deadly germs; a Navy gadget, known as TagMan, can detect in half an hour whether a sample of liquid contains any of several known biological agents. National Guard units, whose normal duties involve dealing with floods and hurricanes, are being retrained as HAZMAT teams in an arrangement between the FBI and the Federal Emergency Management Agency. So many different sectors are now shoring up the nation's defences against megaterrorism, says the government auditor, that it's hard to keep track of the money, let alone know whether it's being spent wisely.

Police and public health officials claim to be so confounded by [anthrax] hoaxes that they hark back to the good old days when the worst they had to deal with was a straightforward bomb scare.

In 1972, President Nixon renounced biological weaponry in the Biological Weapons Convention, which, in an effort to prevent other countries from taking them up, prohibited their development, production and stockpiling. The biological weapons arsenal in Sixties America had been the world's largest and most sophisticated, with 400 biological agents tested, 17 toxic enough for use on the battlefield.

Now, few deny that biological terrorism is a risk; but the speed at which it has come to be regarded as the main threat to U.S. security is as unnerving as the threat itself. And the risk in rushing to meet any new threat by creating new departments of counter-espionage and counter-weapons is that the old practice of deterrence through international treaties may take a back seat.

Few deny that biological terrorism is a risk; but the speed at which it has come to be regarded as the main threat to U.S. security is as unnerving as the threat itself.

"Catastrophic Terrorism" screamed a headline in the November edition of the journal *Foreign Affairs.* The three distinguished authors, John Deutch, a former director of the CIA, Ashton Carter, an ex-Pentagon assistant secretary and Philip Zelikow, a former member of the National Security Council, declared with certainty that "the danger of weapons of mass destruction being used [in acts of terrorism] against America and its allies is greater now than at any time since the Cuban missile crisis of 1962." Any act of catastrophic terrorism, they went on to say, could have the effect of Pearl Harbor, dividing America into a "before" and "after".

The thrust of the article was to call for a grand reorganisation of the Pentagon, the CIA and the FBI in order to eliminate the agency overlaps and gaps between "foreign" and "domestic" terrorism. The authors want to pool intelligence, create new Catastrophic Terrorism Response Offices (dubbed CTROs), and trim the present two dozen agencies with shopping lists for vaccines, gas sniffers and protective clothing down to one, the Pentagon's Defence Department.

While all this goes on, people are losing sight of the fact that, since 1980, the number of Americans killed by terrorists most years has been fewer than 10. (Of course, that toll can suddenly jump. Last summer, for example, the car bombs at the U.S. embassies in Kenya and Tanzania killed 260 people. Before that, in 1995, the bombing of the Oklahoma City Federal Building claimed 168 lives.) Furthermore, there have been only two serious uses of biological weapons this century. The first was during the Second World War, when the invading Japanese Imperial Army experimented with deadly bacteria on Chinese prisoners of war. In 1995, the Japanese cult Aum Shinrikyo attempted to disperse anthrax spores, but no one was killed.

False claims and unjustified fears

Richard Preston, author of *The Cobra Event,* wrote a non-fiction account of the rise of "bioterrorism", which was published in the *New Yorker* in 1997. In that article, Kanatjan Alibekov, the Russian who had been second in command of the weapons section of the Soviet biological weapons programme, appeared for the first time in the press. He had arrived in America in 1992, a year after the fall of communism, and changed his name to Ken Alibek. In Preston's article, he gave details about Biopreparat, the huge plants built for producing biological weapons in Russia. The

1972 Biological Weapons Convention had a loophole: the treaty did not prevent countries from building and keeping in reserve facilities for producing such weapons. This is what the Russians had done. Alibek went further, and claimed that the Soviet plants had been used to produce tons of anthrax, some of which had been genetically engineered to disable the available vaccines. In addition, he claimed that the Russians had experimented with deadly cocktails of smallpox mixed with the Ebola virus, which causes internal haemorrhaging, and Venezuelan equine encephalitis, a virus of the brain.

Various scientific experts were dismissive of Alibek's claims. Dr Peter Jahrling, the chief scientist at the U.S. Army medical research Institute of Infectious Diseases, who was one of Alibek's original debriefers, told the New Yorker, "His talk about chimeras [mixtures] of Ebola is sheer fantasy, in my opinion."

In their article on catastrophic terrorism, Deutch and company mention the proposal by Professor Matthew Meselson, a Harvard University biochemist, and Philip Heymann, his law professor colleague, of an international convention making it a crime for individuals to engage in the production of biological or chemical weapons. The idea would be to deter corporations from assisting in the development of such weapons by making the scientists or CEOs liable for prosecution. If such a treaty had existed and been supported by the U.S. in the Eighties, when Iraq was using poison gas and developing biological weapons, the suppliers and advisers on whom Saddam depended could have been brought to trial.

People are losing sight of the fact that, since 1980, the number of Americans killed by terrorists most years has been fewer than 10.

For a reprieve from the drumbeat warning of the New Threat, one can turn to the autumn issue of American Foreign Policy magazine. In an essay entitled "The Great Terrorism Scare", Ehud Sprinzak, a professor of political science at Jerusalem's Hebrew University, shouts down the voices of doom. The concept of chaos-breeding fanatics in the wake of the Cold War, he says, is simply not supported by the evidence of the past three decades. "Despite the lurid rhetoric, a massive terrorist attack [with weapons of mass destruction] is . . . not even likely," he writes. "Terrorists wish to convince us that they are capable of striking from anywhere at any time, but there is really no chaos. Terrorism involves predictable behavior, and the vast majority of terrorist organizations can be identified well in advance."

But such advice generally falls on deaf ears. In last year's military budget, the Republicans forced an addition of several million dollars for anti-terrorism projects, insisting that America was unprepared to meet potential threats. One thing is certain, then. Come Election 2000, when the politicians are coaxing votes from the good citizens of the United States, anthrax is sure to be high on the agenda.

3

Terrorists Would Be Unlikely to Use Biological or Chemical Weapons

Jonathan B. Tucker and Amy Sands

Jonathan B. Tucker directs the CBW (Chemical and Biological Weapons) Nonproliferation Project at the Center for Nonproliferation Studies, which is part of the Monterey Institute of International Studies in Monterey, California. He has written a few books, including Toxic Terror: Assessing Terrorist Use of Chemical and Biological Weapons. *Amy Sands is the Associate Director of the Center and director of its Monitoring Proliferation Threats Project.*

Despite the few instances in recent years of terrorists employing biological and chemical weapons, it is an extremely uncommon phenomenon. The history of terrorist activities over the last several decades indicates that most extremist groups have neither the motivation nor capabilities to employ such weapons. Examining historical incidents indicates that terrorists seem to prefer the immediate drama of conventional explosions over the drawn-out consequences associated with biological or chemical agents. Most terrorist groups avoid using these devices either because they are unfamiliar with the technologies involved, they fear the potential hazards to their own safety, they have moral limits, or they have other concerns about the consequences of linking such weapons to the political aims of their group. Although it is possible that some fringe organization may use chemical or biological weapons in the future, the current state of alarm is not justified given the historical evidence of terrorist activities.

In a January [1999] speech to the National Academy of Sciences, President Clinton warned that "the enemies of peace realize they cannot defeat us with traditional military means" and are therefore working on "new forms of assault," including chemical and biological weapons (CBW). Responding to this still largely hypothetical threat, the Clinton administration's proposed federal budget for fiscal year 2000 calls for nearly $1.4 billion to protect U.S. citizens against terrorist chemical or biological attacks. That amount would more than double fiscal 1999 spending.

Is such a dramatic increase warranted? Not necessarily. In fact, a variety of factors, including the nerve-gas attack on the Tokyo subway by the Japanese Aum Shinrikyo cult in March 1995, led U.S. officials to overestimate the threat of mass-casualty attacks involving chemical or biological agents. A mid-course correction in U.S. policy is now needed.

At first glance, the threat of chemical and biological terrorism seems to be increasing. Before the late 1980s, the Federal Bureau of Investigation (FBI) typically encountered about a dozen incidents a year involving terrorist threats or actual attempts to acquire or use chemical or biological materials—or (rarely) radiological or nuclear materials.

In 1997, however, the FBI opened 74 investigations involving CBW or nuclear materials, and in 1998, it launched 181 investigations.[1] Nevertheless, about 80 percent of these cases turned out to be hoaxes and the remainder were threats, small-scale attacks, and failed attempts at delivery. In the United States, a mass-casualty attack with a chemical weapon has never occurred—and only one successful incident of biological terrorism has been reported. In 1984, members of the Oregon-based Rajneeshee cult deliberately contaminated restaurant salad bars in the town of The Dalles with salmonella bacteria, affecting 751 people temporarily with a diarrheal illness. Their objective was not to kill people but rather to sicken voters and keep them at home so as to throw the outcome of a local election in the cult's favor.

A whiff of hysteria

U.S. policy-makers and several outside analysts have predicted catastrophic consequences if a terrorist group or an individual—alone or with state sponsorship—ever mounts a major chemical or biological attack. These alarmist scenarios have been based on the potential vulnerability of U.S. urban centers to chemical or biological attack and the growing availability of relevant technology and materials. But these scenarios have not drawn on a careful assessment of terrorist motivations and patterns of behavior.

With more than a hundred terrorist organizations active in the world today, the challenge is to identify groups or individuals who are both motivated and capable of employing chemical or biological agents against civilians. Yet instead of examining historical cases in which terrorists sought to acquire and use such agents, the Clinton administration, as well as many outside analysts, developed their threat assessments and response strategies in an empirical vacuum. Lacking solid data, they fell back on worst-case scenarios that may be remote from reality.

The tendency of U.S. government officials to exaggerate the threat of chemical and biological terrorism has been reinforced by sensational reporting in the press and an obsessive fascination with catastrophic terrorism in Hollywood films, best-selling books, and other mainstays of pop culture. Examples include movies such as *The Rock, Executive Decision, Outbreak,* and *Twelve Monkeys;* novels such as Tom Clancy's *Executive Orders* and *Rainbow Six,* Richard Preston's *The Cobra Event,* and Stephen King's *The Stand;* and episodes of popular television series such as *The X-*

Files, Seven Days, Outer Limits, Millennium, Burning Zone, and even *Chicago Hope.* The sensational depiction of chemical and biological weapons in the popular media seems to have had the unintended effect of making these weapons more attractive to hoaxers, as evidenced by the recent rash of anthrax hoaxes.

Instead of examining historical cases in which terrorists sought to acquire and use [biological and chemical] agents, the Clinton administration, as well as many outside analysts, developed their threat assessments and response strategies in an empirical vacuum.

A few critics have recently begun to question the worst-case assumptions underlying the administration's counterterrorism programs. Science policy analyst Daniel S. Greenberg, writing in the *Washington Post,* criticized what he called "a whiff of hysteria-fanning and budget opportunism in the scary scenarios of the saviors who have stepped forward against the menace of bioterrorism. . . . While a gullible press echoes [their] frightening warnings, there are no independent assessments of the potential for terrorist attacks or the practicality of the proposed responses."[2]

Using more polite language, the General Accounting Office (GAO), the investigative arm of Congress, made a similar point in a preliminary report published in March. The report said that plans developed by the Department of Health and Human Services for "medical consequence management" after a chemical or biological terrorist attack appear to be "geared toward the worst-possible consequences from a public health perspective and do not match intelligence agencies' judgments on the more likely biological and chemical agents a terrorist group or individual might use."

The GAO report concluded: "A sound threat and risk assessment could provide a cohesive roadmap to justify and target spending for medical and other countermeasures to deal with a biological and/or chemical terrorist threat."[3]

Examining the data

It is paradoxical that chemical and biological terrorism has come to occupy such a high position on the worry list of top U.S. government officials when so little is known about the actual threat. At the Center for Nonproliferation Studies at the Monterey Institute of International Studies in Monterey, California, the authors have sought to bridge the gap between anecdote and empirical knowledge. With research assistance from Jason Pate and Diana McCauley, we have compiled a database of 520 global CBW incidents that occurred between 1900 and May 1999.

Our goal in building the database was to help identify which types of terrorist groups were most likely to acquire and use chemical and biological agents, the motives underlying attacks, the choice of agent and target, and other aspects of terrorist behavior.

Although caution is in order when extrapolating from the past to the future, much can be learned from examining actual cases. The Monterey database also permits statistical analysis of the historical record, making it possible to discern patterns over time in the incidence of chemical and biological terrorism. This information should assist policy-makers in developing prudent, cost-effective programs for prevention and response.

The incidents involving chemical or biological agents in the Monterey database include hoaxes, plots, efforts to acquire toxic materials, proven possession of materials, and actual attacks. The incidents have been grouped in two basic categories, terrorist or criminal. There were 282 terrorist cases (54 percent) and 238 criminal cases (46 percent).

We define terrorism as "the instrumental use or threatened use of violence by an organization or individual against innocent civilian targets in furtherance of a political, religious, or ideological objective." Criminal incidents, in contrast, involve extortion, murder, or some other non-political objective. They are not addressed in this article.

Of the 282 incidents grouped in the terrorist category, 263 were selected for analysis because they contained sufficient information to permit cross-case comparison. While most of these incidents took place overseas, 40 percent occurred in the United States.

Contrary to the conventional wisdom about the catastrophic nature of chemical and biological terrorism, actual attacks were few in number, small in scale, and generally produced fewer casualties than conventional bombs.

It is paradoxical that chemical and biological terrorism has come to occupy such a high position on the worry list of top U.S. government officials when so little is known about the actual threat.

A breakdown of the 263 cases between 1900 and last May is eye-opening: 26 percent were hoaxes or pranks, eight percent involved an apparent conspiracy that did not proceed far, four percent involved the attempted acquisition of dangerous materials, 10 percent involved the actual possession of dangerous materials, 21 percent concerned a threatened attack that did not materialize, and only 27 percent (71 incidents) included the actual use of a chemical or biological agent.

Of the actual attacks, 83 percent (59) occurred outside the United States. The largest number of incidents took place in 1995 (16, all non-U.S.) and in 1998 (15, one-third in the United States). In very few cases did the perpetrators seek to inflict mass casualties—defined as 1,000 or more deaths—and in none did they occur.

Among the 71 actual attacks—and again, the coverage is global and the timeframe is 1900 to May of this year—the choice of agent and method of delivery varied considerably. Chemical agents employed included cyanide (by far the most popular), rat poison, VX nerve agent, sarin nerve agent, butyric acid, mercury, and insecticide. Biological agents included anthrax, botulinum toxin, salmonella bacteria, and the HIV virus.

The 71 attacks produced 123 fatalities and 3,774 injuries. Of these totals, the sole U.S. fatality was caused by the use of cyanide-tipped bullets by the Symbionese Liberation Army to assassinate an Oakland, California school superintendent in 1973.

The foreign incidents that inflicted the largest numbers of fatalities were the contamination of drinking water with pesticide by an unknown terrorist group in the Philippines in 1987, causing 19 deaths among new recruits to the Philippine Constabulary on the island of Mindanao, and the use of an unknown poison gas against a Turkish village in 1994, possibly by Kurdish Workers Party (PKK) terrorists, causing 21 deaths.

Contrary to the conventional wisdom about the catastrophic nature of chemical and biological terrorism, actual attacks were few in number, small in scale, and generally produced fewer casualties than conventional bombs.

Of the nonfatal casualties, 1,038 were associated with Aum Shinrikyo's release of sarin nerve agent on the Tokyo subway in 1995.[4]

To date, incidents of chemical or biological terrorism in the United States have inflicted a total of 784 nonfatal injuries, of which 751 were associated with the Rajneeshee food poisoning case. Other major U.S. incidents involving casualties include the 1989 delivery by racial extremists of a package containing a tear-gas bomb to the Atlanta office of the National Association for the Advancement of Colored People, which injured eight; and attacks with butyric acid against abortion clinics in Houston and Florida in 1998, injuring 14 people.

Many of the terrorists implicated in the 71 actual attacks were not traditional terrorist organizations like the Irish Republican Army. Twenty-four attacks were perpetrated by religiously motivated groups, 15 by nationalist-separatist groups, and 12 by single-issue groups such as anti-abortion or animal-rights advocates. The rest were committed by lone terrorists, right-wing or left-wing groups, and unknown actors.

What factors might account for these patterns? Historically, traditional terrorist organizations have eschewed chemical or biological agents for several reasons, including unfamiliarity with the relevant technologies, the hazards and unpredictability of toxic agents, moral constraints, concern that indiscriminate casualties could alienate current or future supporters, and fear that a mass-casualty attack could bring down the full repressive power of the affected government on their heads.

In contrast, individuals and nontraditional groups that have sought to acquire chemical or biological agents tend to be motivated by religious fanaticism, supremacist or anti-government ideology, or millenarian prophecy, and they often have a paranoid, conspiratorial worldview.

Such individuals and groups may view chemical or biological terrorism as a means to destroy a corrupt social structure, to fulfill an apocalyptic prophecy, to exact revenge against evil-doers or oppressors, or as a form of "defensive aggression" against outsiders seen as threats to the group's survival.

Terrorists who contemplate chemical or biological attacks typically lack outside supporters or other moderating influences that might restrain them from engaging in indiscriminate violence. Religiously motivated cults, for example, are cut off from the outside world and are often guided by a charismatic and all-powerful leader, making them less subject to societal norms.

Most of the incidents of chemical or biological terrorism in the United States were grossly ill-conceived and ineffective. Two typical examples: In 1972, an ecoterrorist group called R.I.S.E., led by two students at a community college in Chicago, plotted to wipe out the entire human race with eight different microbial pathogens and then repopulate the world with their own genes.

Their initial scheme was to use aircraft to disperse the disease agents on a global basis, but they eventually scaled down their vision to killing the residents of the five states around Chicago by contaminating urban water supplies. Group members informed the FBI about the plot before it could be carried out, however, and the two ringleaders fled to Cuba.

In 1986, a white supremacist Christian Identity group known as the Covenant, the Sword, and the Arm of the Lord sought to overthrow the federal government and hasten the return of the Messiah. They acquired 30 gallons of potassium cyanide to poison urban water supplies, believing that God would direct the poison to kill only the targeted individuals—nonbelievers, Jews, and blacks living in major cities. Before they could act, however, the FBI penetrated the group and arrested its leaders.

Why toxic weapons?

What specific factors might motivate terrorists to employ chemical or biological agents, as opposed to conventional guns and explosives? Although the desire to inflict mass casualties is one factor, there may be others.

Bombs are appealing to terrorists because of the shock, drama, and cathartic effect of the explosion. Chemical and biological weapons, in contrast, are generally invisible, odorless, tasteless, silent, and insidious. Despite their lack of cathartic power, these weapons evoke deep human anxieties and instill a qualitatively different type of terror.

Nerve agents attack the central nervous system, resulting in seizures, loss of voluntary control, and a gruesome death by respiratory paralysis. Biological agents such as anthrax elicit horrific symptoms of disease such as disfiguring skin eruptions.

These manifestations, and the pervasive threat of contamination with an invisible yet deadly agent, may be more frightening than the sudden trauma of an explosion. Even a chemical or biological attack that killed fewer people than a conventional bomb could have a disproportionate psychological impact.

From an operational standpoint, chemical weapons have both advantages and disadvantages compared with conventional guns and bombs. Nerve agents such as sarin can kill in minutes, and the ability of persistent agents such as mustard or VX to contaminate buildings and people creates the potential for sowing disruption and chaos in an affected urban area.

Disadvantages of chemical weapons are that they are hazardous to handle, unpredictable to disperse in open areas, and can be countered with timely medical intervention such as the administration of antidotes.

With respect to biological agents, terrorists might wish to exploit the ability of certain microorganisms to incapacitate temporarily rather than kill, as in the Rajneeshee cult's use of food-poisoning bacteria. At the other extreme, apocalyptic terrorists seeking to inflict a catastrophic blow against society might employ a highly contagious and lethal agent such as the Ebola virus, which the Aum Shinrikyo cult reportedly sought to acquire in Zaire.[5]

Most of the incidents of chemical or biological terrorism in the United States were grossly ill-conceived and ineffective.

The time lag associated with biological weapons effects also makes them well suited to covert delivery. In recent years, no one has claimed responsibility for the most lethal attacks, in part because countries are pursuing terrorists more aggressively.[6] Terrorists seeking to conceal their involvement and avoid arrest or repression might therefore have a greater incentive to employ biological agents.

For other terrorists, however, the very ambiguity of a biological attack might be perceived as a disadvantage. A sudden epidemic of illness resulting from the deliberate release of a microbial agent—particularly an indigenous strain—could be misinterpreted as a natural outbreak of disease, reducing or eliminating its ability to terrorize. (Public health officials believed that the salmonella outbreak in The Dalles was of natural origin until a former member of the Rajneeshee cult confessed.)

Beyond operational considerations, the choice of poison weapons may be related to deep psychological needs on the part of individual terrorists. From a psychoanalytic perspective, the use of chemical and biological agents may involve the symbolic projection of "poisoned" thoughts and feelings onto "out-group" targets.[7]

On the other hand, the delayed effects of biological agents may reduce the psychological gratification associated with a terrorist attack by creating anxiety and tension until the outcome is known. The Rajneeshees, for example, waited in suspense for two weeks before they learned that the restaurant contaminations had been successful.

Terrorists may also have ideological motivations for employing toxic weapons. Aum Shinrikyo's Shoko Asahara was attracted to sarin because he was an admirer of Nazi Germany, the first country to develop and manufacture nerve agents during World War II.

Quasi-religious terrorist organizations may also have a mystical fascination with poisons and disease. Some Christian Identity extremists, for example, might seek to employ biological agents against their enemies in imitation of biblical descriptions of God's use of plagues—including boils, cattle diseases, and the death of the firstborn son—to punish Pharaoh for stopping the Israelites from leaving Egypt.[8]

Finally, some members of the right-wing patriot movement are fascinated with the protein toxin ricin because it has the glamorous aura of a powerful, "spy weapon" (having been used in 1978 by the Bulgarian Secret Service to assassinate a dissident living in London). Ricin is also mistakenly believed to be an untraceable poison that will enable perpetrators to evade arrest and prosecution. In 1991, for example, four members of the Minnesota Patriots Council acquired ricin and discussed assassinating Internal Revenue Service officials, a U.S. deputy marshal, and local law enforcement officers. The FBI had penetrated the group, however, and arrests were made before any attacks were carried out.

It is also important to distinguish between discrete and indiscriminate CBW attacks. Just because chemical and germ agents are often described as "weapons of mass destruction," it does not follow that the ability to inflict mass casualties is an intrinsic property. Key variables in determining the impact of a CBW terrorist attack are the quantity of agent employed and the means of dissemination.

Members of Aum Shinrikyo, for example, used VX to assassinate enemies of the cult by spraying the nerve agent from a hypodermic syringe into the victim's face. This small-scale use of a chemical weapon for assassination is clearly different from releasing a ton of nerve agent from an aircraft over a major city.

Technical hurdles

One reason there have been so few successful examples of chemical or biological terrorism is that carrying out an attack requires overcoming a series of major technical hurdles: gaining access to specialized chemical-weapon ingredients or virulent microbial strains; acquiring equipment and know-how for agent production and dispersal; and creating an organizational structure capable of resisting infiltration or early detection by law enforcement.

Many of the microorganisms best suited to catastrophic terrorism—virulent strains of anthrax or deadly viruses such as smallpox and Ebola—are difficult to acquire. Further, nearly all viral and rickettsial agents are hard to produce, and bacteria such as plague are difficult to "weaponize" so that they will survive the process of delivery.

As former Soviet bioweapons scientist Ken Alibek wrote in his recent memoir, *Biohazard*, "The most virulent culture in a test tube is useless as an offensive weapon until it has been put through a process that gives it stability and predictability. The manufacturing technique is, in a sense, the real weapon, and it is harder to develop than individual agents."[9]

The delayed effects of biological agents may reduce the psychological gratification associated with a terrorist attack by creating anxiety and tension until the outcome is known.

The capability to disperse microbes and toxins over a wide area as an inhalable aerosol—the form best suited for inflicting mass casualties—requires a delivery system whose development would outstrip the technical capabilities of all but the most sophisticated terrorists. Not only is the dissemination process for biological agents inherently complex, requiring specialized equipment and expertise, but effective dispersal is easily disrupted by environmental and meteorological conditions.

A large-scale attack with anthrax spores against a city, for example, would require the use of a crop duster with custom-built spray nozzles that could generate a high-concentration aerosol cloud containing particles of agent between one and five microns in size. Particles smaller than one micron would not lodge in the victims' lungs, while particles much larger than five microns would not remain suspended for long in the atmosphere.

Not only is the dissemination process for biological agents inherently complex, requiring specialized equipment and expertise, but effective dispersal is easily disrupted by environmental and meteorological conditions.

To generate mass casualties, the anthrax would have to be dried and milled into a fine powder. Yet this type of processing requires complex and costly equipment, as well as systems for high biological containment. Anthrax is simpler to handle in a wet form called a "slurry," but the efficiency of aerosolization is greatly reduced.

(A low-tech terrorist might stage a chemical or biological attack in an enclosed space such as a subway station, as did Aum Shinrikyo, but fewer people would be harmed than in an open-air attack against a city.)

Contamination of an urban water system is also beyond the capability of most terrorists because a huge volume of a chemical or biological agent would be needed to overcome the effects of dilution and chlorination. In contrast, a small-scale attack on restaurant food or a water tank would be more feasible.

So far the FBI has not obtained evidence that any terrorist organization has succeeded in building a device capable of delivering a mass-casualty biological attack. Aum Shinrikyo, for example, failed in 10 known attempts in Japan to conduct biological attacks with either anthrax or botulinum toxin.[10]

Despite the cult's vast financial resources (approximately $1 billion) and access to trained scientists, it was unable to overcome the technical hurdles associated with the acquisition of a virulent strain, cultivation of the agent, and efficient delivery.

Terrorists groups must also be capable of evading detection by law enforcement until after they have carried out an attack. While lone psychopaths motivated to use chemical or biological weapons may avoid the notice of the police, their technical and resource limitations make them unlikely to be capable of acts of mass-casualty terrorism.

Conversely, several terrorist organizations that have sought in the past to acquire chemical or biological agents have been infiltrated by the FBI or betrayed by informants before they could implement an effective attack.

As a result of these various constraints, crude or "low-tech" delivery methods, such as those employed by Aum Shinrikyo and the Rajneeshee cult, are likely to remain the most common forms of chemical or biological terrorism. These methods are potentially capable of inflicting at most tens to hundreds of fatalities—within the destructive range of a high-explosive bomb—but not the mass death envisioned by alarmist scenarios.

Assessing the threat

The historical record suggests that only a tiny minority of terrorists will be motivated to carry out an indiscriminate chemical or biological attack, and that few if any of this subset will possess the necessary technology and expertise to actually accomplish it.

Thus, the most likely incidents of chemical or biological terrorism in the future will involve hoaxes and relatively small-scale attacks. Moreover, although chemical or biological agents are often termed "weapons of mass destruction," some terrorists have sought to employ such agents in a limited manner to assassinate individuals.

Of course, governments cannot afford to be complacent about the potential for high-casualty chemical and biological attacks by terrorists who gain access to military-grade agents and delivery systems—particularly if they receive assistance from a state. A state sponsor that believed it could shield its identity through intermediaries might take the risk, particularly in a crisis or during a war. Incidents of state-sponsored chemical or biological terrorism, however, have been exceedingly rare. All have involved special-operations forces rather than independent terrorist organizations, probably because states fear losing control over proxy groups. States may also be deterred from sponsoring terrorism by the likelihood of severe retaliation if the source of the attack were to become known.

Nevertheless, ad hoc or "transnational" terrorist organizations, such as the group that bombed the World Trade Center, have inspired growing concern because they may be only loosely affiliated with a state sponsor and hence less constrained.

Terrorists with ample financial resources might also seek to purchase technical know-how by recruiting scientists formerly employed by countries with advanced chemical or biological programs, such as the Soviet Union, South Africa, or Iraq.

Contamination of an urban water system is also beyond the capability of most terrorists because a huge volume of a chemical or biological agent would be needed to overcome the effects of dilution and chlorination.

Further comparative analysis of historical cases should help refine the profile of terrorist groups and individuals most likely to acquire and use chemical and biological agents. If motivations and patterns of behavior associated with this form of terrorism are better understood, it might be possible for intelligence and law enforcement agencies to narrow the "bandwidth" of individuals and organizations considered to be of greatest concern. That, in turn, would permit a more efficient application of intelligence resources, which might otherwise be stretched unproductively over too broad a field of suspects.

The potential threat posed by lone terrorists and small splinter groups, who can easily slip through the surveillance net, may lower confidence in the ability to prevent acts of chemical or biological terrorism before they occur. Even so, better profiling of terrorist groups should enhance the ability of law enforcement officials to assess the credibility of terrorist threats and to manage the current epidemic of anthrax hoaxes.

Historical analysis of patterns of behavior of CBW terrorists, such as the choice of agent and delivery system, can also help improve the effectiveness of medical countermeasures and other consequence-management activities.

Although some planning for worst-case scenarios is justified, the types of chemical and biological terrorism against which federal, state, and local planning should be primarily directed are small- to medium-scale attacks.

Such a threat assessment is not the stuff of newspaper headlines, but the historical record surely justifies it.

Notes

1. Judy Parker-Tursman, "FBI Briefed on District's Terror Curbs," *Pittsburgh Post-Gazette,* May 5, 1999.

2. Daniel S. Greenberg, "The Bioterrorism Panic," *Washington Post,* March 16, 1999, p. A21.

3. U.S. General Accounting Office, "Combating Terrorism: Observations of Biological Terrorism and Public Health Initiatives," Statement of Henry L. Hinton, Jr., Assistant Comptroller General, National Security and International Affairs Division, GAO/T-NSAID-99-112, March 16, 1999, p. 3.

4. U.S. Public Health Service, Office of Emergency Preparedness, Proceedings of the Seminar on Responding to the Consequences of Chemical and Biological Terrorism (Washington, D.C.: USPHS, 1995), pp. 2–32.

5. David E. Kaplan and Andrew Marshall, *The Cult at the End of the World* (New York: Crown Publishers, 1996), p. 97.

6. Bruce Hoffman, "A New Kind of Terrorism: Silence is Deadlier," *Los Angeles Times,* Aug. 18, 1996, p. M1.

7. Jerrold M. Post, "Terrorist Psycho-Logic: Terrorist Behavior as a Product of Psychological Forces," in Walter Reich, ed., *Origins of Terrorism: Psychologies, Ideologies, Theologies, States of Mind* (Washington, D.C.: Woodrow Wilson Center Press, 1990), pp. 25–40.

8. Jessica Stern, *The Ultimate Terrorists* (Cambridge, Mass.: Harvard University Press, 1999), p. 70.

9. Ken Alibek with Stephen Handelman, *Biohazard* (New York: Random House, 1999), p. 97.

10. Sheryl WuDunn, Judith Miller, and William J. Broad, "How Japan Germ Terror Alerted World," *New York Times,* May 26, 1998, pp. A1, A10.

4

Countermeasures to Biological and Chemical Terrorism Warrant Government Funding

W. Seth Carus

W. Seth Carus is a senior research professor at the National Defense University. He is also the author of Ballistic Missiles in the Third World *and* The Poor Man's Atomic Bomb? Biological Weapons in the Middle East.

An increased fear of biological or chemical terrorism has prompted the Clinton administration to raise federal spending on countermeasures and emergency response to attacks by such weapons. Although there have been few cases of this type of terrorism to warrant funding, the administration's concern is appropriate. The possibility of such attacks and their nightmarish consequences should motivate any government to take severe precautions. And with at least a dozen countries capable of making biological and chemical weapons, the budget for protecting against an attack may be justified. However, since much of the potential threat is based on speculation, government officials should scrutinize exactly how the budget is allocated and whether all of the countermeasures are effective and cost efficient responses to the predicted threat.

On July 14 [1999], a bipartisan commission headed by former CIA Director John Deutch will release its report on the readiness of the United States to deal with weapons of mass destruction. While the Deutch commission expresses concerns about loose Russian nukes and Chinese missile exports, it's also alarmed by the prospect of terrorists armed with biological weapons. Among the commission's nightmarish scenarios is an anthrax attack on a crowded subway system that sends

6,000 people to the hospital. "These events have not taken place," the panel intones, "but they could."

The Deutch commission is the latest example of how nervous Washington has become about bioterrorism. Senior Clinton administration officials are convinced that bioterrorism poses an imminent and serious, perhaps cataclysmic, danger. Their budget reflects that conviction: the fiscal year 2000 budget proposal includes $1.4 billion for both chemical and biological terrorism responses, double the 1999 spending levels. This includes the Department of Health and Human Services's Bioterrorism Initiative, whose budget ballooned from $14 million in fiscal year 1998 to $158 million [in 1999]; and the fiscal year 2000 budget calls for $230 million. In addition, the FBI, the Federal Emergency Management Agency, and the Departments of Agriculture, Defense, Energy, and Justice have smaller initiatives.

A difficult threat to assess

Yet it's far from clear how grave the bioterrorism threat really is. Thanks to the dearth of empirical data on bioterrorism, it's nearly impossible to make accurate threat assessments. Since 1945, only about 23 terrorist groups are known to have even thought about using biological weapons—and the evidence to support some of these allegations is extremely thin. Of the 23 groups, only seven actually possessed a biological agent, and only four of them tried to use those weapons in any fashion. The only successful act of biological terrorism occurred in 1984, when the Rajneeshee, a cult group then based in rural Oregon, used biological agents to make 751 people sick as part of a plot to influence the outcome of an election. By contrast, the Aum Shinrikyo cult in Japan devoted considerable effort to developing biological weapons. The cult tried to spread anthrax and botulinum toxin approximately ten times between 1990 and 1995, but it was totally unsuccessful. Japanese officials reportedly believe that Aum used a harmless vaccine strain of anthrax and never produced botulinum toxin.

Just because terrorists haven't had much interest in, or success with, biological weapons in the past doesn't mean they won't use them in the future.

To be sure, just because terrorists haven't had much interest in, or success with, biological weapons in the past doesn't mean they won't use them in the future. Reports of varying quality suggest that [Saudi terrorist leader] Osama Bin Ladin, the Islamic Jihad [Middle Eastern organization], and the Kurdish PKK [Kurdish Workers Party operating in the Middle East] have shown some interest in bioterrorism during the past few years. Similarly, some domestic terrorist groups have also reportedly demonstrated an interest. But, with rare exceptions—such as the two men belonging to the Minnesota Patriots Council who, in 1995, were found guilty of producing the ricin toxin as part of a plot to kill government officials—there is no compelling evidence that any of these groups, foreign or domestic, have actually acquired biological agents or even know how to use them. Indeed, the evidence suggests that terrorists are unlikely to acquire biological weapons unless they get them from a state sponsor.

Even if we don't know much about the terrorists, there is a large and authoritative body of knowledge about the use and effects of biological agents—and it is scary.

The only surefire bioterrorism threat assessments we do have are, for the most part, about the now-ubiquitous anthrax hoaxes. Since March 1998, there have been more than 150 publicly reported incidents of someone falsely claiming that a victim had been exposed to anthrax. A wide array of hoax perpetrators have discovered that, for the price of a first-class stamp or a call from a pay phone, they can generate considerable fear and confusion. Anti-abortion activists have disrupted dozens of abortion clinics in this way; and, apparently in retaliation, anti-abortion demonstrators themselves have been victims of similar hoaxes. Students, some as young as twelve, have sent anthrax threats to their schools. One man interrupted his bankruptcy proceeding by telephoning in an anthrax threat; another man tried the same ploy to get out of work early.

Catastrophic potential

So, if it's impossible to accurately gauge the bioterrorism threat, why is the U.S. government so worried? One major reason is that the scenarios generated by security analysts to illustrate the potential dangers of biological agents are so scary. The only problem is that, since there's so little empirical data about bioterrorism, the scenarios are necessarily works of fiction; scenario writers, limited only by their imaginations, are free to dream up almost any kind of threat. Thus, even a mildly creative analyst can dream up threats that overwhelm any reasonable set of response capabilities. Yet, such scenarios provide little insight into the types of agents that might be used or how they would be used, because they are not based on a factual understanding of terrorist motivations or capabilities. Rather, they reflect the biases of the scenario writer.

But the government's fear of bioterrorism isn't completely unfounded. Even if we don't know much about the terrorists, there is a large and authoritative body of knowledge about the use and effects of biological agents—and it is scary. This technical data, much of it obtained prior to the cancellation of the U.S. offensive biological program in 1969, demonstrates that it's possible to place large populations at risk by releasing appropriately prepared pathogens into the air. Even relatively small quantities of biological agents can have catastrophic results: a panel of World Health Organization experts calculated that 50 kilograms of anthrax released over a city of half a million people would kill 95,000 and incapacitate another 125,000. Some experts believe that, pound for pound, biological weapons are potentially more lethal than thermonuclear warheads.

Despite the Biological Weapons Convention prohibition on possession of biological weapons, the U.S. intelligence community apparently believes that at least a dozen countries may have offensive biological weapons programs. Among those countries are two of the permanent members of the U.N. Security Council—China and Russia—and all six countries on the State Department's list of state supporters of terrorism—Iran, Iraq, Libya, North Korea, Sudan, and Syria. Significantly, Iran, Iraq, and North Korea are the three countries most likely to confront the United States militarily. While there's no current evidence that any of these countries has given biological weapons to any terrorist group, it's not difficult to imagine circumstances in which such a transfer could happen.

Moreover, the absence of evidence regarding terrorists' capabilities to employ biological agents is not necessarily comforting. Collecting intelligence on biological weapons programs—even on state programs—is extremely difficult. For instance, the intelligence community knew nothing of Aum Shinrikyo's efforts to develop and use biological agents until after the Tokyo sarin attacks. The first indication of terrorist possession of biological warfare capabilities may only come when those capabilities are used.

In the absence of credible threat assessments, there is no way to quantify the seriousness of the threat or to calculate the resources needed to respond. Nor is it possible to predict with confidence which specific biological agents terrorists might adopt, how they might employ them, or where the potential targets might be located. This makes it difficult to properly allocate resources and suggests caution in developing responses.

Appropriate responses

Therefore, the focus of our bioterrorism response policy ought to be on programs that make sense even if the nation never experiences a single bioterrorism attack. One such program is the Center for Disease Control's (CDC) Epidemic Intelligence Service (EIS), which investigates unusual disease outbreaks. It was created in the early 1950s specifically because of concerns that foreign powers might use biological weapons against the United States. The CDC has sent EIS officers to investigate thousands of disease outbreaks, and, although the EIS has never identified a foreign biowarfare attack on the United States, most public health experts believe the service is a valuable and cost-effective part of the nation's public health infrastructure.

From this perspective, many aspects of the Clinton administration's plans are quite sensible. The first indication of a bioterrorism attack is likely to be the appearance of sick people, which justifies efforts to improve the nation's disease-surveillance systems to detect and then responds promptly to outbreaks. Public health laboratories need to be upgraded, both to identify biological agents and to ensure that results are quickly circulated. Considering that the nation's public health infrastructure has been woefully underfunded for decades, these initiatives would make considerable sense, even if there were no bioterrorism threat.

Other activities that the administration wants to fund are so small, and the potential scientific benefits so large, that the expenditure is justified. Thus, spending $24 million for the National Institutes of Health to research likely threat agents and develop new treatments for them makes considerable sense. Providing training and equipment to the country's largest cities as part of the National Domestic Preparedness program is also good policy. Even if no terrorist attacks occur, the training will enhance local capabilities to respond to hazardous materials incidents.

The focus of our bioterrorism response policy ought to be on programs that make sense even if the nation never experiences a single bioterrorism attack.

Unfortunately, some programs the administration wants to fund will provide tangible benefits only if a terrorist actually uses a biological agent, and, thus, they require more scrutiny. This is true for devices designed to provide rapid detection and identification of biological agents in the field. The medical stockpile program, through which the CDC will create reserves of antibiotics and certain vaccines, is more problematic. Although the CDC is finding ways to reduce the cost of stocking antibiotics, the vaccines are extremely costly and could be useless. In the absence of adequate threat assessments, it's impossible to know what types of agents terrorists might use; a stockpile of anthrax and smallpox vaccines won't do much good against tularemia or Marburg.

In the final analysis, there is a compelling need to enhance the nation's ability to contend with the possibility of biological terrorism. The threat, however, is less compelling and not as imminent as often claimed. And the threat is most likely to originate from a foreign government's bioweapons program. Given these uncertainties, we have almost no ability to predict the character of a bioterrorism attack. Therefore, greater effort needs to be made to justify spending on bioterrorism responses to ensure that the resources are spent wisely.

5

The Media Direct
U.S. Policy Regarding
Biological and
Chemical Weapons

Stephen S. Hall

Stephen S. Hall is the science editor for the New York Times Sunday Magazine, *and author of such biological studies as* Invisible Frontiers: The Race to Synthesize a Human Gene *and* A Commotion in the Blood: Life, Death, and the Immune System.

Science fiction novels, such as Richard Preston's *The Cobra Event,* have done much to exacerbate fears over America's susceptibility to attacks by biological and chemical weapons. President Bill Clinton's alarmist call to budget hundreds of millions of dollars to safeguard the United States against such attacks in the year 2000 came suspiciously on the heels of his reading *The Cobra Event.* Yet many experts agree that the catastrophic events described in these works of science fiction could never occur; and the small-scale scares involving chemical or biological agents that have actually taken place all failed to cause mass deaths. Money set aside to protect against hypothetical attacks based in fiction would be better spent battling common, real diseases that claim hundreds of thousands of lives each year.

At a time when Hollywood producers jet in to script White House speeches, it comes as no surprise that politics often gets conflated with entertainment. But it may be surprising to learn that the nation's controversial new policy on bioterrorism was apparently inspired, at least in part, by a work of fiction.

Bill Clinton's enthusiasm for "black biology" arose largely from his reading of a novel called *The Cobra Event,* according to an account in the *New York Times* last August. The author, Richard Preston, has written sev-

Reprinted from "Science-Fiction Policy," by Stephen S. Hall, *Technology Review,* November/December 1998, vol. 101, no. 6. Reprinted with permission of *Technology Review* conveyed through Copyright Clearance Center, Inc.

eral estimable nonfiction books, including *First Light*, a superb account of contemporary astronomy. But Preston is best known for *The Hot Zone,* a best seller that introduced the lay public to the ebola virus.

Scarifying prose

The Hot Zone describes a 1989 outbreak of ebola virus in a monkey population in Reston, Va., which—readers were led to believe—seemed destined to lead to a biological holocaust in the surrounding suburbs. To be fair, infectious disease experts were concerned that humans might indeed become infected. But the hair-raising narrative tends to smudge a salient, deflating fact: A number of humans had been exposed to the monkey virus for up to six weeks before authorities even got wind of the problem, whereas the incubation time for ebola is two to 21 days. Four animal handlers did show signs of infection with the virus—but none became ill. The account represents prodigious reporting, told in taut scarifying prose, all in the service of . . . a nonevent.

It may be surprising to learn that the nation's controversial new policy on bioterrorism was apparently inspired, at least in part, by a work of fiction.

The Cobra Event is similarly scary, and also schizophrenic. Half of it reads like fiction (a better than average page-turner and light-years more sophisticated than *The Andromeda Strain*) and half like nonfiction (written with the clarity and authority of Preston's other nonfiction books). The plot, boiled down to basics, has a deranged scientist testing a genetically engineered bioweapon in New York City and Washington, D.C. This fictional virus combines the worst traits of smallpox, common cold virus, and a prolifically replicating insect virus, and comes seasoned with a genetic glitch that causes the self-mutilating disorder known as Lesch-Nyhan syndrome. People begin to die horrible deaths; their brains liquify and they gnaw off their own lips, fingers and tongues.

Implausible scenario

Cobra is a clever concoction, but is it plausible? "No way in hell it would work," says C.J. Peters of the Centers for Disease Control and Prevention in Atlanta, perhaps the world's leading expert on "hot" viruses. Norton Zinder, a molecular biologist at Rockefeller University who has worked on viruses for half a century, agrees that a recombinant virus like Cobra "has no probability of working," and goes much further. "There is no evidence that biological warfare is a useful weapon. These guys," he says, referring not only to popularizers but also to Defense Department bioterrorism experts in search of funding, "are making a living out of scaring people."

It's become commonplace to suggest in the media (as *New Scientist* did not long ago) that "it's only a matter of time before bioterrorists strike." But as the *New York Times* reported last May, they already have—

and no one noticed. The Japanese cult Aum Shinrikyo launched at least nine biological attacks in the early 1990s, using either anthrax spores or the microbe that causes botulism; all such efforts failed. Smallpox and anthrax are legitimate concerns, but Aum Shinrikyo's difficulties underscore an often-overlooked point—bioweapons are difficult to make, even more difficult to deploy, and much more unpredictable than a bomb. Furthermore, laboratory strains of viruses and bacteria are often coddled in ideal culture conditions, but may not be so robust in the real world.

Yet the "threat industry," as Zinder calls it, used fear to distort our policy priorities. I asked C.J. Peters to give me a quick-and-dirty estimate of total global human fatalities attributable to ebola, Lassa, and other hemorrhagic viruses each year; his conservative educated guess was around 6,000, though possibly 10 times as high. By contrast, 3 million people perished from tuberculosis and perhaps 2.7 million from malaria in 1997, according to World Health Organization statistics; 2 million children die from enteric diseases each year, 2 million die from respiratory infections, and more than 800,000 kids under 5 die from measles. (All those illnesses, by the way, are treatable and in some cases preventable.) Ebola, *The Hot Zone* virus, claims approximately 25 lives a year.

Fiction influencing policy

Goaded by the merchants of fear, the Clinton administration has requested $300 million in next year's budget to begin stockpiling antibiotics, step up vaccine research and train state and local authorities to deal with a chemical or biological weapons attack.

I like roller coasters as much as the next guy, but the vicarious pleasure of fear belongs in the province of entertainment, not public policy. The devils we already know—TB, malaria, measles and so on—have exacted many orders of magnitude more human suffering and mortality than the devil we have yet to see. Instead of spending countless millions on antibiotics and vaccines that might never be used, I'd like to see the government spend that money on development of better vaccines for common diseases and reforms of the economics that cripple drug development and distribution for the developing world.

6

An Attempt to Destroy Chemical Weapons Goes Awry

Kevin Whitelaw, Warren P. Strobel, and Brian Duffy

Kevin Whitelaw and Brian Duffy are reporters for U.S. News & World Report. *Duffy and fellow journalist Jim McGee co-authored* Main Justice: The Men and Women Who Enforce the Nation's Criminal Laws and Guard Its Liberties. *Strobel is a former White House correspondent for the* Washington Times *and is currently a senior editor for* U.S. News & World Report. *He is the author of* Late-Breaking Foreign Policy: The News Media's Influence on Peace Operations.

In August 1998, American missiles fired from ships in the Red Sea struck their intended target, the El Shifa pharmaceutical plant in Sudan. The U.S. government claims the attack was in retaliation for the bombings of U.S. embassies in Kenya and Tanzania which occurred two weeks prior to the strike. The alleged mastermind behind the attacks on the embassies was Saudi terrorist Osama bin Laden, and the U.S. believed there was a link between bin Laden and the El Shifa plant. In fact, the White House contends the El Shifa plant was actually a chemical weapons facility that could supply bin Laden's organization with weapons of mass destruction intended primarily to be used against U.S. targets.

Yet after the attack, no evidence has surfaced to substantiate the government's claims that the plant was indeed manufacturing chemical weapons. It appears that the attack may have been more of a warning against Sudan because its government allegedly shelters terrorists. Whatever its intention, the rash act backfired on the United States as the Sudanese gained worldwide sympathy by portraying themselves as the victim of unjust U.S. aggressions.

On August 20 last year [1998], 13 American cruise missiles slammed into a dusty pharmaceutical plant in Sudan. The strike, the White House said, was in retaliation for the bombings of the U.S. embassies in

Reprinted from "It Was a Direct Hit, but Was It the Right Target?" by Kevin Whitelaw, Warren P. Strobel, and Brian Duffy, *U.S. News & World Report*, August 16–23, 1999, vol. 127, no. 7. Copyright ©1999 by U.S. News & World Report. Reprinted with permission. Visit us at our website www.usnews.com for additional information.

Kenya and Tanzania two weeks earlier. But many of the U.S. intelligence analysts who keep tabs on African affairs were kept out of the loop, and they were skeptical that the plant, known as El Shifa, was a chemical weapons facility connected to the alleged terrorist Osama bin Laden. That was the charge leveled by top U.S. officials at the time. Responding to government critics of the strike, the CIA invited several analysts to a presentation by the agency's scientific experts. They explained how U.S. intelligence had obtained a soil sample containing EMPTA, which is used to make VX nerve gas. The meeting turned into a disaster. "It didn't convince anyone," says an official who was present. "The iron curtain came down after that." It's still down today. The administration's evidence against El Shifa remains secret—even to most American officials. What is known isn't encouraging. In the strike's immediate aftermath, an informal review conducted by the State Department's Bureau of Intelligence and Research failed to turn up a single piece of evidence linking El Shifa to chemical weapons or bin Laden. The bureau was discouraged from even reporting its findings. Says one U.S. intelligence official, "To this day, I don't know" why they chose El Shifa.

Misguided retribution

Unlike the mistaken bombing of the Chinese Embassy in Belgrade in May, the El Shifa bombing stems from more than an intelligence failure. A staunch anti-Sudan policy left some senior State Department and National Security Council aides inclined to believe the worst about the Islamic government in Khartoum, government officials say. There's plenty of bad news, to be sure. Sudan has been accused of repeated human-rights violations in its long-running civil war. It has been blamed for sparking a deadly famine by cutting off aid flights. It allegedly harbors terrorists.

But what about El Shifa? Some current and former U.S. officials say Washington developed a harder line against Sudan in 1995, after intelligence agencies passed along reports of a possible assassination plot against then National Security Adviser Anthony Lake. The alleged culprits were Sudanese-based terrorists. The threat was never substantiated, but around the same time, the U.S. Embassy in Khartoum was closed, virtually cutting off the flow of firsthand information from Sudan. From then on, some officials say, the anti-Sudan line in Washington got harder. U.S. policy makers dismissed many of Sudan's overtures about peace negotiations outright. And when Sudan finally signed the chemical weapons treaty in May, the United States ignored it. Joe Sala, a former Africa expert at the State Department, says this philosophy is simple: "It's Sudan, and we don't like them."

Elusive evidence

The decision to bomb El Shifa was made by fewer than a dozen top U.S. officials. This meant that experts on both Sudan and chemical weapons were not consulted about the government's evidence. Over the past year, White House officials, including National Security Adviser Sandy Berger, have backed away from their charge that El Shifa was actually producing chemicals for weapons as opposed to being a storage or transshipment point. But Clinton advisers insist they have seen no new evidence to undercut their conclusion that the plant was linked to bin Laden and the Iraqi chemical weapons program. Another factor, says one official, "tipped the scales": It could be struck with little risk of civilian casualties.

In the strike's immediate aftermath, an informal review conducted by the State Department's Bureau of Intelligence and Research failed to turn up a single piece of evidence linking El Shifa to chemical weapons or [terrorist Osama] bin Laden.

Still, virtually everything the administration said publicly about El Shifa in the days after the attack has turned out to be wrong. At the time of the attack, the United States did not know who owned the plant. No evidence has surfaced to support claims that the plant was heavily secured. And government spokesmen misspoke when they said El Shifa did not produce legitimate pharmaceutical products, apparently unaware the plant had a United Nations license to ship drugs to Iraq.

The key evidence touted by U.S. officials was a soil sample taken by a CIA operative from the grounds of El Shifa that supposedly tested positive for EMPTA. But tests by outside labs of samples taken after the bombing have found no trace of EMPTA or any of its components. And the House intelligence committee was told that the CIA's original soil sample was so small it was used up in the initial testing.

U.S. officials have been unable to publicly back up their assertions that El Shifa's owner, Saleh Idris, a Saudi Arabian businessman, is linked to bin Laden. After the strike, the Treasury Department promptly froze $24 million of his assets, alleging links to terrorists. Idris denied the charges and sued the government. An intermediary spoke with White House counsel Charles Ruff, who apparently helped release the assets in May after obtaining an intelligence briefing.

An investigation by the security firm Kroll Associates, paid for by Idris, turned up no evidence of any links between Idris and bin Laden except very tenuous connections through distant third parties. Idris told *U.S. News* that he plans to file a second lawsuit "very soon" seeking compensation for his $30 million factory. "Everyone on the globe knows this was a mistake," he says.

Mission backfired

In the end, Sudan has benefited from the U.S. strike, gaining sympathy from many other governments. But the Sudanese government remains its own worst enemy. Khartoum banned aid flights to two war-torn regions again last month, putting 150,000 people at risk of starvation. And a U.N. team was sent to Sudan last week to investigate the government's alleged use of chemical weapons against the rebels.

In Washington, House and Senate intelligence committees are continuing to investigate the decisions leading to the attack. The strike represents "a real lowering of the threshold for military action against countries with whom we have a disagreement," says one congressional aide with access to intelligence reports. But if anything, Congress is even more anti-Sudan than the administration. Both houses have overwhelmingly condemned Sudan within the past two months and called for U.S. support to the rebels. For now, any comprehensive scrutiny of the missile strike remains unlikely.

7

Decreasing U.S. Intervention Overseas Will Reduce the Threat of Terrorist Attacks

Ivan Eland

Ivan Eland is the Director of Defense Policy Studies at Washington D.C.'s Cato Institute.

According to a Department of Defense study there is a strong correlation between U.S. intervention in foreign affairs and the number of terrorist acts against Americans. In the past, such acts typically involved conventional weapons and claimed relatively few lives, and were therefore deemed annoyances rather than catastrophes. However, now that biological weapons are garnering worldwide attention, the government should rightfully fear the possibility that terrorists may begin to use such devices against American soil. This potential threat could be minimized if the United States would change its foreign policy to avoid meddling in international disputes in which America's vital interests are not at stake. By removing terrorists' motivation, the U.S. could escape retaliatory attacks involving such catastrophic weapons of mass destruction.

S everal government reports have emphasized the need for increased national attention to the defense of the American homeland. That mission has not been prominent since the 1950s, but the proliferation of technology for creating weapons of mass destruction—chemical, biological, or nuclear—has reawakened interest in protecting the homeland.

According to a study completed for the Department of Defense (DoD), historical data show a strong correlation between American involvement in international situations and terrorist attacks against the U.S. Once regarded as pinpricks by great powers, attacks by terrorist groups could be catastrophic for the American homeland. Terrorists can obtain the technology for weapons of mass destruction and will have fewer qualms about using them to cause massive casualties. Assistant Sec-

Reprinted from "Defending Other Nations: The Risk to America's Homeland," by Ivan Eland, *USA Today* magazine, September 1998, vol. 127, no. 2640. Copyright ©1998 by the Society for the Advancement of Education. Reprinted with permission.

retary of Defense for Reserve Affairs Deborah Lee maintains that such events are almost certain to occur. It will be extremely difficult to deter, prevent, detect, or mitigate such actions.

As a result, there has been a dramatic change in the strategic environment for the U.S. Even the weakest terrorist group can cause massive destruction in the homeland of a superpower. Yet, the U.S. continues to threaten to intervene or actually intervene militarily in foreign conflicts all over the globe that are irrelevant to American vital interests—for example, in the ongoing crisis with Iraq over weapons inspections. Such an interventionist foreign policy provokes hostility from certain factions or groups within the affected countries.

Military restraint

To satisfy what should be the first priority of any security policy—protecting the homeland and its people—the U.S. should adopt a policy of military restraint. That would entail intervening only as a last resort when truly vital interests are at stake. To paraphrase Anthony Zinni, the commander of American forces in the Middle East, the U.S. should avoid making enemies, but should not be kind to those that arise. According to a statement made by Secretary of Defense William Cohen in the Department of Defense's November, 1997, report, Proliferation: Threat and Response: "With advanced technology and a smaller world of porous borders, the ability to unleash mass sickness, death, and destruction today has reached a far greater order of magnitude. A lone madman or nest of fanatics with a bottle of chemicals, a batch of plague-inducing bacteria, or a crude nuclear bomb can threaten or kill tens of thousands of people in a single act of malevolence.

"These are not far-off or far-fetched scenarios. They are real—here and now. Weapons of mass destruction already have spread into new hands. As the new millennium approaches, the United States faces a heightened prospect that regional aggressors, third-rate armies, terrorist cells, and even religious cults will wield disproportionate power by using—or even threatening to use—nuclear, biological, or chemical weapons against our troops in the field and our people at home.

Historical data show a strong correlation between American involvement in international situations and terrorist attacks against the U.S.

"America's military superiority cannot shield us completely from this threat. Indeed, a paradox of the new strategic environment is that American military superiority actually increases the threat of nuclear, biological, and chemical attack against us by creating incentives for adversaries to challenge us asymmetrically. These weapons may be used as tools of terrorism against the American people."

Although the U.S.'s military superiority contributes to the increased likelihood of a terrorist attack by nuclear, biological, or chemical means, it is the interventionist foreign policy that the military power carries out that is the real culprit. That point was acknowledged by the Defense Science Board study for Undersecretary of Defense for Acquisition and Technology Jacques S. Gansler, DoD's Responses to Transnational Threats: "As part of its global superpower position, the United States is called upon frequently to respond to international causes and deploy forces around the world. America's position in the world invites attack simply because of its presence. Historical data show a strong correlation between U.S. involvement in international situations and an increase in terrorist attacks against the United States."

Lee put it even more strongly: "Counterterrorism specialists define the problem not as a question of if, but of when and where such attacks will take place." Biological and chemical weapons can be produced easily and inexpensively employing commercially available raw materials and technologies in comparatively small facilities used for developing mundane commercial products. There are many such facilities capable of making chemical and biological weapons in the world. Nuclear material is harder to get than biological or chemical precursors, but it is becoming more available because of the deteriorating conditions in the nations of the former Soviet Union.

In addition to the ease with which terrorists can obtain weapons of mass destruction, they have become more willing and able to inflict massive casualties using such weapons. Seth Carus, an expert on biological terrorism at the National Defense University, notes that, "First, there are terrorists who want to kill large numbers of people. There have been such groups in the past, but there appear to be a growing number who want mass casualties. The World Trade Center and Oklahoma City bombings both were conducted by people who had no compunction about mass killing. Second, the technological sophistication of the terrorist group is growing."

A terrorist attack with weapons of mass destruction—almost impossible to deter, detect in a timely fashion, prevent, or mitigate—against a target in the U.S. could make the World Trade Center attack, or even the Oklahoma City bombing, seem minor by comparison. Casualties could range from the tens of thousands to the millions. According to Cohen, five pounds of the biological weapon anthrax could annihilate half the population of Washington, D.C.

Thus, the only viable way to reduce the very real threat of such an attack is to reduce U.S. interference in the disputes and conflicts of other nations. According to Matthew Meselson, a geneticist at Harvard University and co-publisher of the journal The *CBW Conventions Bulletin,* which tracks chemical and biological arms, "The best protection would be if we didn't have any angry people or countries in the world." Thus, military intervention should be confined to the rare cases when American vital interests are at stake.

Impossibility of eliminating the threat

The intense interest of the international community and the most relentless inspections in history have been focused on Iraq's weapons of mass destruction programs. The spotlight has been much greater than that under the normal enforcement of international agreements designed to stem proliferation. Even so, the international community never will be assured that all of Saddam Hussein's weapons and the facilities needed to make them have been uncovered and destroyed. In fact, the sole reason the international community knew about Saddam's biological weapons program was that his son-in-law defected and revealed its existence.

Despite the extensive efforts to determine the location of Iraqi weapon stockpiles and production facilities, information is far from complete. "Put bluntly, we don't really know what Iraq has. And that's the heart of the problem," indicates Charles Duelfer, deputy chief of the UN's Special Commission in charge of inspecting suspected Iraqi sites. Biological weapons, for instance, can be manufactured quickly and hidden, and they can be destroyed quickly if in danger of being found by inspectors.

To satisfy what should be the first priority of any security policy—protecting the homeland and its people—the U.S. should adopt a policy of military restraint.

Even military action—bombing—is unlikely to wipe out Iraq's chemical and biological weapons labs, which are small, mobile, and easily hidden. During the most recent crisis with Iraq, U.S. Air Force officials admitted that they did not know the location of the remaining facilities and that any successful air strikes would have been by accident.

In the unlikely event that the international community did succeed in destroying all existing stockpiles and facilities, Saddam could produce more chemical and biological agents using readily available commercial technologies after the inspectors left. Gen. Henry Shelton, chairman of the Joint Chiefs of Staff, admitted how easy it would be for Iraqi technicians to transform a hospital, veterans clinic, or fertilizer plant into a facility for making anthrax or mustard gas weapons: "You can convert one of them quickly and resume making chemical or biological weapons. One day he's making fertilizer, the next day chemical [weapons], and the next day fertilizer."

If Saddam can conduct those weapons programs under such close scrutiny, other rogue nations—and especially terrorist groups sponsored by such countries or acting independently—are likely to be at least as successful in doing so. Even if inspectors became a permanent fixture in Iraq, the international community does not have the energy or resources to conduct such ongoing inspections in every nation it suspects of developing—or harboring terrorists that are developing—chemical or biological weapons.

Thus, Iraq and other rogue states are likely to possess biological or chemical weapons. In fact, it is unclear why the U.S. has singled out Iraq. Syria, Libya, and Iran also are likely to have either chemical or biological weapons. However, Iraq and the other rogue nations have no missiles that could carry biological or chemical weapons far enough to strike the U.S. Even if they did, they probably would hesitate to launch them against America because the U.S. could detect the origin of such missiles and retaliate with nuclear weapons.

Any sort of U.S. military action against those nations designed to destroy biological and chemical weapons would fail (as noted above) and might even be counterproductive. In retaliation for American military strikes, any rogue state could sponsor a terrorist attack against the U.S. using chemical or biological agents. Richard Butler, head of the UN Special Commission's weapons inspection team in Iraq, asserted that everyone wonders what kind of delivery system that nation may have for biological weapons, yet the best delivery system would be a suitcase left in the Washington subway.

The operations of terrorist groups (and the nations that sponsor them) are notoriously hard to penetrate, even with human intelligence agents. Furthermore, during the Cold War, such U.S. capabilities eroded as the intelligence agencies relied more on the high technology of electronic and satellite systems to monitor the U.S.S.R. Such collection systems are not good at detecting chemical and biological manufacturing and storage sites. Thus, the Defense Science Board argues that the government's primary efforts should be in "consequence management"—mitigating the effects of chemical and biological attacks with detectors, protective clothing, vaccines, and medical treatment—because prevention and interdiction through intelligence efforts are likely to be too difficult.

Detecting and mitigating the effects of an attack with weapons of mass destruction is a near impossible task. It is easy to smuggle the materials needed to make them into the U.S. The quantities are small, and America's borders are thousands of miles long.

America is vulnerable

Once the nuclear, biological, or chemical material has been smuggled into the U.S., several dissemination methods are possible. While a bomb would be needed to make nuclear material achieve critical mass, it is possible to design a nuclear weapon that is small enough to fit in a satchel. Barring that method, any ship or vehicle could be used to deliver a crude nuclear bomb into a large metropolitan area. Even a conventional truck bomb could be used to spread medical radiological waste over a wide area.

A truck with a sprayer could be used to deliver toxic chemical agents. Along with placing plastic bags filled with sarin nerve agent in the Tokyo subway, a Japanese religious cult used this method. Chemical agents could be dispersed from a crop-dusting aircraft or rooftop sprayer. Although it is somewhat more complex to disseminate biological agents than chemical agents, the same methods of delivery could be used.

The only viable way to reduce the very real threat of [biological] attack is to reduce U.S. interference in the disputes and conflicts of other nations.

Detecting a biological or chemical attack in time to save the thousands, tens of thousands, or even millions of people who otherwise would die is a daunting task. For a biological incident, the first indication that an attack has occurred may show up a couple of days after the release of the germs—when people start coming to hospital emergency rooms with respiratory problems. By the time the symptoms are visible, however, it often is too late to administer an antidote. Vaccines for specific agents are available, but it is impractical to vaccinate the entire population for all possible biological agents, and terrorists could bioengineer new organisms that are resistant to vaccines or antidotes. For chemical incidents, decontaminating victims or giving them antidotes must be done quickly or the patient will die. For both biological and chemical incidents, decontamination often is slow and the large quantities (tons) of the specific antidote needed for each of the many possible agents are likely to be expensive and either not at hand or unavailable rapidly. Buying protective clothing for 270,000,000 Americans to shield them from chemical and biological attack would be expensive and might not be very effective.

George Washington and Thomas Jefferson believed that, if the U.S. stayed out of the affairs of other countries, those nations, in turn, would have less of an excuse to get involved in the affairs of America.

The independent National Defense Panel is pessimistic that any defense against terrorist attacks using weapons of mass destruction would be viable: "No defense will ever be so effective that determined adversaries, such as terrorists bent on making a political statement, will not be able to penetrate it in some fashion." Even one such penetration by terrorists could be catastrophic.

Comments by Joshua Lederberg, a Nobel Laureate at the National Academy of Sciences, about bioterrorism easily could apply to other weapons of mass terror: "There is no technical solution to the problem of biological weapons. It needs an ethical, human, and moral solution if it's going to happen at all. Don't ask me what the odds are for an ethical solution, but there is no other solution. But would an ethical solution appeal to a sociopath?"

Noninterventionist foreign policy

Because it is extremely difficult to deter, prevent, or mitigate an attack by terrorists using weapons of mass destruction, the U.S. should lessen the chances that such groups would be motivated to conduct such an attack in retaliation for American intervention abroad. This can be done by using military force overseas just when U.S. vital interests are at stake. This policy was followed for the better part of the first 165 years of the nation's history. George Washington and Thomas Jefferson believed that, if the U.S. stayed out of the affairs of other countries, those nations, in turn, would have less of an excuse to get involved in the affairs of America. Only during the 50 years of the Cold War was this policy turned on its head in favor of intervention anywhere and everywhere all over the world in the name of fighting global communism. The Cold War is over, but U.S. foreign policy remains on autopilot. The U.S. military is busier than it was during the Cold War, even though no rival superpower exists to capitalize on "instability" anywhere in the world. The interventionist foreign policy that was an aberration in American history now seems like the norm.

The National Defense Panel, in arguing for a re-emphasis on homeland defense, noted that "protecting the territory of the United States and its citizens from 'all enemies both foreign and domestic' is the principal task of government." Yet, by protecting everyone in the world, the U.S. is endangering its own citizens. America must abandon its policy of being a military nanny in every area of the world. The U.S. government's excessively interventionist foreign policy undermines what should be its first priority in order to reap amorphous gains by "enhancing stability" or "promoting democracy" in far away places.

As the Senate's Committee on Governmental Affairs noted in its publication the *Proliferation Primer*, the U.S.—like Gulliver—has become a vulnerable giant. Are such questionable interventions overseas really worth the potential catastrophic consequences to the American people? The answer is a resounding "No."

8

The Migration of Russian Biological Weapons Experts Is a Serious Threat

Jonathan B. Tucker

Jonathan B. Tucker directs the CBW (Chemical and Biological Weapons) Nonproliferation Project at the Center for Nonproliferation Studies, which is part of the Monterey Institute of International Studies in Monterey, California. He has written a few books, including Toxic Terror: Assessing Terrorist Use of Chemical and Biological Weapons.

During the Cold War, the Soviet Union's vigorous biological warfare program was of grave concern to the United States. Now that the Soviet Union has collapsed, America must worry over the potential leaks of that "bioweapon" knowledge and technology to foreign governments or terrorist organizations. Of prime consideration are the number of newly-unemployed Soviet scientists who could defect to foreign countries willing to pay for their expertise in creating biological weapons. American authorities also fear that these scientists may smuggle biological agents or technology out of the country and into the hands of rogue states or terrorist groups willing to use them. To counter the potential migration, the United States is funding programs in Russia to keep Soviet scientists employed in peaceful research, sometimes in collaboration with American scientists. The U.S. government hopes that such measures will persuade Soviet researchers to remain in their native land and allow U.S. experts unprecedented access to previously guarded Soviet knowledge.

For nearly two decades, the former Soviet Union and then Russia maintained an offensive biological warfare (BW) program in violation of an international treaty, the 1972 Biological and Toxin Weapons Convention. In addition to five military microbiological facilities under the control of the Soviet Ministry of Defense (MOD), a complex of nearly 50 scientific institutes and production facilities worked on biological weapons

Reprinted from "Bioweapons from Russia: Stemming the Flow," by Jonathan B. Tucker, *Issues in Science and Technology*, Spring 1999, pp. 34–38, vol. 15, no. 3. Copyright ©1999 by the University of Texas at Dallas, Richardson, TX. Reprinted with permission.

under the cover of the Soviet Academy of Sciences, the Ministry of Agriculture, the Ministry of Health, and an ostensibly civilian pharmaceutical complex known as Biopreparat. The full magnitude of this top-secret program was not revealed until the defection to the West of senior bioweapons scientists in 1989 and 1992.

Today, the legacy of the Soviet BW program, combined with continued economic displacement, poses a serious threat of proliferation of related know-how, materials, and equipment to outlaw states and possibly to terrorist groups. The three primary areas of concern are the "brain drain" of former BW specialists, the smuggling of pathogenic agents, and the export or diversion of dual-use technology and equipment. Although the U.S. government is expanding its nonproliferation activities in this area, far more needs to be done.

The Soviet BW complex

The nonmilitary Soviet BW complex comprised 47 facilities, with major R&D centers in Moscow, Leningrad, Obolensk, and Koltsovo (Siberia) and standby production facilities in Omutninsk, Pokrov, Berdsk, Penza, Kurgan, and Stepnogorsk (Kazakhstan). According to Kenneth Alibek (formerly known as Kanatjan Alibekov), the former deputy director for science of Biopreparat, a total of about 70,000 Soviet scientists and technicians were employed in BW-related activities in several state institutions. Biopreparat employed some 40,000 people, of whom about 9,000 were scientists and engineers; the MOD had roughly 15,000 employees at the five military microbiological institutes under its control; the Ministry of Agriculture had about 10,000 scientists working on development and production of anticrop and antilivestock weapons; the institutes of the Soviet Academy of Sciences employed hundreds of scientists working on BW-related research; and additional researchers worked on biological weapons for the Anti-Plague Institutes of the Soviet Ministry of Health, the Ministry of Public Culture, and other state institutions. Even the KGB had its own BW research program, which developed biological and toxin agents for assassination and special operations under the code name Flayta ("flute"). Ph.D.-level scientists were in the minority, but technicians acquired sensitive knowledge about virulent strains or the design of special bomblets to be used to disseminate biological agents.

The legacy of the Soviet BW program, combined with continued economic displacement, poses a serious threat of proliferation of related know-how, materials, and equipment to outlaw states and possibly to terrorist groups.

According to defector reports, Soviet military microbiologists did research on about 50 disease agents, created weapons from about a dozen, and conducted open-air testing on Vozrozhdeniye Island in the Aral Sea. Beginning in 1984, the top priority in the five-year plan for the Biopreparat research institutes was to alter the genetic structure of known pathogens such as plague and tularemia to make them resistant to Western antibiotics. Soviet scientists were also working to develop entirely new classes of biological weapons, such as "bioregulators" that could modify human moods, emotions, heart rhythms, and sleep patterns. To plan for the large-scale production of BW agents in wartime, Biopreparat established a mobilization program. By 1987, the complex could produce 200 kilograms of dried anthrax or plague bacteria per week if ordered to do so.

The specter of brain drain

In April 1992, Russian President Boris Yeltsin officially acknowledged the existence of an offensive BW program and issued an edict to dismantle these capabilities. As a result of Yeltsin's decree and the severe weakness of the Russian economy, the operating and research budgets of many biological research centers were slashed, and thousands of scientists and technicians stopped being paid. From the late 1980s to 1994, for example, the State Research Center for Virology and Biotechnology ("Vector") in Koltsovo lost an estimated 3,500 personnel. Similarly, between 1990 and 1996, the State Research Center for Applied Microbiology in Obolensk lost 54 percent of its staff, including 28 percent of its Ph.D. scientists.

This drastic downsizing raised fears that former Soviet bioweapons experts, suffering economic hardship, might be recruited by outlaw states or terrorist groups. In congressional testimony in 1992, Robert Gates, then director of the U.S. Central Intelligence Agency, expressed particular concern about "bioweaponeers" whose skills have no civilian counterpart. According to Andrew Weber, special advisor for threat reduction policy at the Pentagon, about 300 former Biopreparat scientists have emigrated from the former Soviet Union to the United States, Europe, and elsewhere, but no one knows how many have moved to countries of BW proliferation concern. Despite the lack of information about the whereabouts of former bioweapons scientists, some anecdotes are troubling. For example, in his 1995 memoir, former Obolensk director Igor V. Domaradskij reported that in March 1992, desperate for work, he offered to sell his services to the Chinese Embassy in Moscow. He made a similar offer in May 1993 to Kirsan Ilyumzhin, president of the Kalmyk Republic within the Russian Federation, but reportedly received no response to either inquiry.

Some directors of former BW research centers have sought to keep their top talent intact by dismissing more junior scientists and technicians. Yet because of the Russian economic crisis, which worsened in August 1998 with the collapse of the ruble, even high-level scientists are not being paid their $100 average monthly salaries.

Iranian recruitment efforts

Iran has been particularly aggressive about recruiting former Soviet bioweapons scientists. The *London Sunday Times* reported in its August 27, 1995 edition that by hiring Russian BW experts, Iran had made a "quantum leap forward" in its development of biological weapons by proceeding directly from basic research to production and acquiring an effective delivery system. More recently, an article published in the December 8, 1998 edition of the *New York Times* alleged that the government of Iran has offered former BW scientists in Russia, Kazakhstan, and Moldova jobs paying as much as $5,000 a month, which is far more than these people can make in a year in Russia. Although most of the Iranian offers were rebuffed, Russian scientists who were interviewed said that at least five of their colleagues had gone to work in Iran in recent years. One scientist described these arrangements as "marriages of convenience, and often of necessity."

According to the *New York Times*, many of the initial contacts with the former Biopreparat institutes were made by Mehdi Rezayat, an English-speaking pharmacologist who claims to be a "scientific advisor" to Iranian President Mohammed Khatami. Iranian delegations who visited the institutes usually expressed interest in scientific exchanges or commercial contacts, but two Russian scientists said that they had been specifically invited to help Iran develop biological weapons. Of particular interest to the Iranians were genetic engineering techniques and microbes that could be used to destroy crops. In 1997, for example, Valeriy Lipkin, deputy director of the Russian Academy of Sciences Institute of Bioorganic Chemistry, was approached by an Iranian delegation that expressed interest in genetic engineering techniques and made tempting proposals for him and his colleagues to come and work for a while in Tehran. Lipkin states that his institute turned down the Iranian proposals.

Nevertheless, evidence collected by opposition groups within Iran and released publicly in January 1999 by the National Council of Resistance indicates that Brigadier General Mohammed Fa'ezi, the Iranian government official responsible for overseas recruitment, has signed up several Russian scientists, some of them on one-year contracts. According to this report, Russian BW experts are working for the Iranian Ministry of Defense Special Industries Organization, the Defense Ministry Industries, and the Pasteur Institute. Moreover, on January 26, 1999, the Moscow daily *Kommersant* reported that in 1998, Anatoliy Makarov, director of the All-Russia Scientific Research Institute of Phytopathology, led a scientific delegation to Tehran and gave the Iranians information related to the use of plant pathogens to destroy crops.

Novel forms of brain drain

Although the scale and scope of the Russian brain drain problem are hard to assess from unclassified sources, early assumptions about the phenomenon appear to have been wrong. Some scientists have moved abroad, but the predicted mass exodus of weapon specialists has not materialized. One reason is that few Russians want to leave family and friends and live in an alien culture, even for more money. Some evidence suggests, however, that brain drain may be taking novel forms.

First, foreign governments are not merely recruiting Russia's underpaid military scientists to emigrate to those countries but are enlisting them in weapons projects within Russia's own borders. Former BW scientists living in Russia have been approached by foreign agents seeking information, technology, and designs, often under the cover of legitimate business practices to avoid attracting attention.

Second, some weapons scientists could be moonlighting by modem: that is, supplementing their meager salaries by covertly supporting foreign weapons projects on the margins of their legitimate activities. This form of brain drain is based on modern communication techniques, such as e-mail and faxes, which are available at some of the Russian scientific institutes.

Iran has been particularly aggressive about recruiting former Soviet bioweapons scientists.

Third, bioweapons scientists could be selling access to, or copies of, sensitive documents related to BW production and techniques for creating weapons. Detailed "cookbooks" would be of great assistance to a country seeking to acquire its own biological arsenal. Despite Yeltsin's edict requiring the elimination of all offensive BW materials, a 1998 article in the Russian magazine *Sovershenno Sekretno* alleged that archives related to the production of biological agents have been removed from the MOD facilities at Kirov and Yekaterinburg and from a number of Biopreparat facilities and put in long-term storage.

Diversion of agents and equipment

Another disturbing possibility is that scientists could smuggle Russian military strains of biological agents to outlaw countries or terrorist groups seeking a BW capability. Obtaining military seed cultures is not essential for making biological weapons, because virulent strains can be obtained from natural sources. According to Alibek, however, Soviet bioweapons specialists modified a number of disease agents to make them particularly deadly: for example, by rendering them resistant to standard antibiotic therapies and to environmental stresses.

Because a seed culture of dried anthrax spores could be carried in a sealed plastic vial the size of a thumbnail, detecting such contraband at a border is almost impossible. Unlike fissile materials, biological agents do not give off telltale radiation nor do they show up on x-rays. The article in *Sovershenno Sekretno* claims that "Stealing BW is easier than stealing change out of people's pockets. The most widespread method for contraband transport of military strains is very simple—within a plastic cigarette package."

Smuggling of military strains out of secure facilities in Russia has already been alleged. Domaradskij's memoir states that in 1984, when security within the Soviet BW complex was extremely high, a scientist named Anisimov developed an antibiotic-resistant strain of tularemia at the military microbiological facility in Sverdlovsk (now Yekaterinburg). He was then transferred to a Biopreparat facility, but because he wanted to get a Ph.D. degree for his work on tularemia, he stole a sample of the Sverdlovsk strain and brought it with him to his new job. When accused of the theft, Anisimov claimed innocence, but analysis of his culture revealed that it bore a biochemical marker unique to the Sverdlovsk strain. Despite this compelling evidence, senior Soviet officials reportedly covered up the incident.

The more than 15,000 viral strains in the culture collection at the Vector virology institute include a number of highly infectious and lethal pathogens such as the smallpox, Ebola, and Marburg viruses, the theft or diversion of which could be catastrophic. Because of current concerns about the possible smuggling of military seed cultures, the U.S. government is spending $1.5 million to upgrade physical security and accounting procedures for the viral culture collection at Vector and plans to invest a similar amount in enhanced security at Obolensk.

Another troubling development has been the export by Russia of dual-use technology and equipment to countries of BW proliferation concern. For example, in the fall of 1997, weapons inspectors with the United Nations Special Commission on Iraq (UNSCOM) uncovered a confidential document at an Iraqi government ministry describing lengthy negotiations with an official Russian delegation that culminated in July 1995, in a deal worth millions of dollars, in the sale of a 5,000-liter fermentation vessel. The Iraqis claimed that the fermentor would be used to manufacture single-cell protein (SCP) for animal feed, but before the 1991 Persian Gulf War, Iraq used a similar SCP plant at a site called Al Hakam for large-scale production of two BW agents, anthrax and botulinum toxin. It is not known whether the Russian fermentor ordered by Iraq was ever delivered.

Efforts to stem brain drain

To counter the recruiting of Russian BW scientists by Iran and other proliferant states, the United States has begun to expand its support of several programs designed to keep former BW experts and institutes gainfully employed in peaceful research activities. The largest effort to address the brain drain problem is the International Science and Technology Center (ISTC) in Moscow. Funded by private companies and by the governments of Russia, the United States, the European Union, Japan, South Korea, and Norway, the ISTC became operational in August 1992. Since then, the center has spent nearly $190 million on projects that include small research grants (worth about $400 to $700 a month) so that former weapons scientists can pursue peaceful applications of their expertise.

Stealing BW is easier than stealing change out of people's pockets. The most widespread method for contraband transport of military strains [of virulent toxins] is very simple—within a plastic cigarette package.

The initial focus of the ISTC was almost exclusively on nuclear and missile experts, but in 1994 the center began to include former BW facilities and scientists. Because of dual-use and oversight concerns, this effort proceeded slowly; by 1996, only 4 percent of the projects funded by the ISTC involved former bioweapons specialists. In 1998, however, the proportion of biologists rose to about 15 percent, and they now constitute 1,055 of the 17,800 scientists receiving ISTC grants. Although the stipends are far less than what Iran is offering, U.S. officials believe that the program is attractive because it allows Russian scientists to remain at home. Even so, the current level of funding is still not commensurate with the gravity of the BW proliferation threat.

Another ISTC program, launched in 1996 by the U.S. National Academy of Sciences (NAS) with funding from the U.S. Department of Defense, supports joint research projects between Russian and U.S. scientists on the epidemiology, prophylaxis, diagnosis, and therapy of diseases associated with dangerous pathogens. Eight pilot projects have been successfully implemented, and the Pentagon plans to support a number of additional projects related primarily to defenses against BW. The rationale for this effort is to stem brain drain, to increase transparency at former Soviet BW facilities, to benefit from Russian advances in biodefense technologies, and—in the words of a 1997 NAS report—to help reconfigure the former Soviet BW complex into a "less diffuse, less uncertain, and more public-health oriented establishment."

Other programs to engage former Soviet BW expertise are being funded by the U.S. Defense Advanced Research Projects Agency, the Agricultural Research Service of the U.S. Department of Agriculture, and the U.S. Department of Energy's Initiatives for Proliferation Prevention Program, which promotes the development of marketable technologies at former weapons facilities. The U.S. Department of Health and Human Services is also interested in supporting Russian research on pathogens of public health concern. In fiscal year 1999, the Clinton administration plans to spend at least $20 million on scientist-to-scientist exchanges, joint research projects, and programs to convert laboratories and institutes.

Without Western financial support, security at the former BW institutes could deteriorate to dangerous levels.

Some conservative members of Congress oppose collaborative work between U.S. and Russian scientists on hazardous infectious diseases because they could help Russia to keep its BW development teams intact. But supporters of such projects such as Anne Harrington, Senior Coordinator for Nonproliferation/Science Cooperation at the Department of State, counter that Russia will continue to do research on dangerous pathogens and that it is in the U.S. interest to engage the key scientific experts at the former BW institutes and to guide their work in a peaceful direction. Collaborative projects have greatly enhanced transparency by giving U.S. scientists unprecedented access to once top-secret Russian laboratories. Moreover, without Western financial support, security at the former BW institutes could deteriorate to dangerous levels.

Given the continued BW proliferation threat from the former Soviet Union, the United States and other partner countries should continue and broaden their engagement of former BW research and production facilities in Russia, Kazakhstan, Uzbekistan, and Moldova. Because the line between offensive and defensive research on BW is defined largely by intent, however, ambiguities and suspicions are bound to persist. To allay these concerns, collaborative projects should be structured in such a way as to build confidence that Russia has abandoned offensively oriented work. In particular, it is essential that scientific collaborations with former BW experts and facilities be subjected to extensive oversight, including regular unimpeded access to facilities, personnel, and information.

The United States should encourage and assist Russia to strengthen its export controls on sales of dual-use equipment [that could be used to manufacture pharmaceuticals or biological weapons] to countries of BW proliferation concern.

At the same time, the United States should continue to work through bilateral and multilateral channels to enhance the transparency of Russia's past offensive BW program and its current defensive activities. An important first step in this direction was taken on December 17, 1998, when U.S. and Russian military officials met for the first time at the Russian Military Academy of Radiological, Chemical and Biological Defense in Tambov and agreed in principle to a series of reciprocal visits to military biodefense facilities in both countries. The U.S. government should explore ways of broadening this initial constructive contact. Finally, the United States should encourage and assist Russia to strengthen its export controls on sales of dual-use equipment to countries of BW proliferation concern.

ISTC programs are pioneering a new type of arms control based on confidence building, transparency, and scientific collaboration rather than negotiated agreements and formal verification measures. This approach is particularly well suited to the nonproliferation of biological weapons, which depends to a large extent on individual scientist's decisions not to share sensitive expertise and materials.

9

A Nuclear Arsenal Is Needed to Counter a Biological Weapons Threat

David C. Gompert

David C. Gompert is vice president of the Rand Corporation in Santa Monica, California, where he runs the National Security Research Division. He served as senior director for Europe and Eurasia on the National Security Council staff during the Bush administration. This article is an expansion of a paper written for the Strategic Forum of the National Defense University. It is based on ideas he developed with former Rand colleagues, Dean Wilkening and Kenneth Watman.

During the Cold War a nuclear arsenal was a means to deter the Soviet Union from launching a nuclear strike against the United States. Now that the Soviet Union has disintegrated, America should not stand down its nuclear deterrence. Indeed, even if the United States no longer fears nuclear attack, it should have great concern over attack by other weapons of mass destruction. The United States should utilize its nuclear superiority as a tool to dissuade terrorist nations or other superpowers from using biological weapons against U.S. targets. And by maintaining the potential of a first-use policy, America will warn rogue states that the response to a biological weapons attack would be swift and catastrophic.

Although nuclear arms control negotiations have stalled in recent years, U.S. and Russian nuclear arsenals have been greatly reduced. That suggests that nuclear weapons now have—and will continue to have—a reduced role in world affairs. That is surely a good thing. But precisely what that role will be remains unclear.

Many arms control enthusiasts, and undoubtedly the majority of the *Bulletin's* readers, believe that a declaratory policy of "no-first-use" of nuclear weapons—pledging never to use nuclear weapons except in retaliation against a nuclear attack—is a critical step in assuring nuclear peace.

But that would be a risky strategy. Attempting to lower the danger of nuclear violence through no-first-use would weaken the fear that nuclear weapons produce. If that fear helps prevent mass casualties from new and comparably dreadful weapons, we may not want to nullify it.

We have some experience with the fear of nuclear war. During the Cold War, it was used by the United States to engender caution and to produce stability. Had it not been for that fear, the twentieth century might have had three world wars instead of two.

The nuclear standoff—parity between arsenals large enough to assure mutual destruction—negated the nuclear threat and thus the likelihood of nuclear war. But simultaneously, the United States negated that negation by threatening to use nuclear weapons to block aggression by conventional Soviet forces. Fearing for their way of life, Americans risked nuclear war to buttress the status quo.

But the world has been transformed. The American way of life is no longer threatened; rather, it is on the march. Because the main current of change—globalization—promotes its interests and ideals, the United States no longer seeks to freeze the international situation. U.S. technological and conventional military capabilities instill confidence in means other than nuclear weapons to thwart conventional aggression.

Should the United States therefore embrace no-first-use, the opposite of the U.S. Cold War doctrine on the use of nuclear weapons? Should it disengage nuclear weapons altogether from international security and military strategy, relying on them solely to deter nuclear war? Is this humankind's chance to eradicate nuclear fear, even if the weapons themselves cannot be eradicated?

Regrettably, the answer is no.

Although the threat of a nuclear response to a conventional attack is no longer crucial to U.S. strategy, the United States still needs nuclear weapons to deter a nuclear attack. But it must also, I believe, present a threat of nuclear retaliation to deter a biological attack, which could be as deadly, and which might not be deterred by the threat of U.S. conventional retaliation.

In this century, the United States should aim to reduce the importance and attractiveness of nuclear weapons and it should delegitimize their use in response to conventional threats. But it must also sharpen nuclear deterrence against biological weapons. The United States could do this by stating that it would use nuclear weapons only in retaliation for attacks with weapons of mass destruction (WMD).

Such a policy of no-first-use of weapons of mass destruction would better support U.S. and international security than either a policy of no-first-use of nuclear weapons or the current official policy, which in its ambiguity rules out nothing.

The new era

The conditions that once led the United States to rely on nuclear weapons to deter aggression, shore up its strategic position, and perpetuate international stability no longer exist. Now predominant and unthreatened, the United States is no longer a status-quo power. Rather, it is a beneficiary of international change, which yields economic liberalization, democratization, integration, and improved security.

Most of the world's economic output, technological capacity, and military power lie within the circle of free-market democracies—the Americas, Europe, East Asia—a community that continues to expand. The success of the past two decades, beyond any expectation, has largely dispelled the dread of systemic instability.

Even though there is continuing uncertainty regarding the future of the U.S.-Chinese relationship, few analysts believe that China will become a Soviet-style threat in the next century. The Soviet Union sought to build its own system in isolation from—and as an alternative to—the Western world, and it failed. The Chinese have learned that lesson well. They seek to join the West. They are concerned with changing China, not the world.

Attempting to lower the danger of nuclear violence through no-first-use would weaken the fear nuclear weapons produce. If that fear helps prevent mass casualties from new and comparably dreadful weapons, we may not want to nullify it.

More broadly, the trend toward democratization and globalization is reducing the danger of the sort of world war that helped make the twentieth century so appallingly bloody, and that caused the United States to engage nuclear weapons in the cause of equilibrium.

The prime mover of the favorable course of world politics is information technology, which is propagating investment, reform, and accountable government. It is also increasingly crucial to power, including military power.

A nation's ability to create and apply information technology depends on its openness and its involvement in the world economy. Authoritarian nations, even large ones, that rely on encrusted state economic power will be handicapped in the dominant technology of the new era. The world's most successful powers in the twenty-first century will likely be free-market democracies with convergent interests and outlooks, as is now the case.

Some scholars of geopolitics believe that clinging to its top ranking should be America's paramount objective. But in reality, the United States has an increasing stake in the success of the other great powers—Japan, the European Union, and yes, China.

More and more, U.S. foreign policy is designed not to block others but to collaborate and grow with them. The United States need not fear any challenger to the extent that it must exploit the fear of general nuclear war to help contain it, as it did with the Soviet Union.

Although the U.S. nuclear arsenal is the world's best, it is, thankfully, no longer an emblem of American power. Compared to U.S. technological and economic leadership, nuclear weapons neither distinguish the United States nor reflect the essence of its strength. Indeed, diluting further the symbolic and political significance of nuclear weapons cannot hurt—and it may help—American interests and image.

Non-nuclear military capabilities, in contrast, are integral to American power in the new era. The forces of the United States can defend its interests wherever required. The American defense budget is again on the rise. Because the United States is the first to exploit information technology strategically, its conventional military superiority is growing.

U.S. forces are being networked, making them more lethal, less vulnerable, and capable of integrated operations. Although the extreme one-sidedness of the recent U.S.-led NATO campaign against Serbia may set unrealistic standards for future combat, the ability of the United States to destroy an adversary's capacity to fight, without suffering high casualties, is apparent.

The idea that the United States would risk—indeed, start—nuclear war to avoid military defeat is far-fetched if not bizarre. For as far into the future as one can imagine, these basic conditions will remain.

Redefining threats

With its technological lead, its growing conventional military superiority, the absence of a mortal enemy, its stature in other forms of power, and its confidence in the face of change, the United States could decouple nuclear weapons from its military strategy and foreign policy without endangering the nation. But before redefining the purpose of nuclear weapons, we must ask if there are any emerging non-nuclear threats that warrant the threat, or the option, of a nuclear response.

Like most technologies, dangerous or benign, biochemical technology is spreading as the global economy integrates. Consequently, U.S. forces, U.S. allies, and eventually U.S. citizens will be vulnerable to attack with biological and chemical weapons delivered by long-range missiles or by clandestine means.

Of the two types, chemical and biological, the latter weapons present the greater danger of casualties on a nuclear scale. Ten kilograms of anthrax is at least as deadly as a 10-kilogram nuclear explosive, and it is cheaper, easier to assemble, and more portable.

The United States could [sharpen deterrence of biological attack] by stating that it would use nuclear weapons only in retaliation for attacks with weapons of mass destruction.

While chemical weapons are more likely to be used to disrupt U.S. military operations, biological weapons pose terrible and lingering dangers to the general population, much like strategic nuclear weapons.

The most immediate concern is that rogue states, lacking other options, might threaten to use biological weapons against U.S. troops in a local war. The United States can partly neutralize this threat by exploiting information technology—dispersing its forces and striking accurately from afar. But determined enemies will then resort to longer-range means to threaten U.S. forces, allies, and territory.

Try as it might to stop the spread of these weapons, the United States must prepare to prevent or defend against their use. But defense alone, with antimissile and counterforce weapons, cannot make American forces and citizens entirely safe from lethal biological agents. Deterrence is crucial.

Defense alone, with antimissile and counterforce weapons, cannot make American forces and citizens entirely safe from lethal biological agents. Deterrence is crucial.

A common argument is that U.S. conventional military superiority—the ability to render an adversary defenseless—should suffice to deter the use of weapons of mass destruction. However, an enemy may already be receiving the full brunt of U.S. conventional strikes when it opts to threaten biological attack. Indeed, the most plausible reason why a rogue state would threaten to use weapons of mass destruction is that the United States has already unleashed its conventional might to defeat local aggression.

Given that, the threat of U.S. conventional reprisal presumably would be ineffective. And because the United States has forsworn biological and chemical weapons, deterrence could depend critically on the threat to retaliate with nuclear weapons. That, of course, would be contradicted by a nuclear no-first-use policy.

The countries whose WMD programs most worry the United States are rogue states such as Iraq, North Korea, and Iran. Because the aim of such states is to deter a U.S. conventional attack, it follows that an American pledge not to use nuclear weapons first, even if they had faith in it, would not diminish their interest in nuclear weapons.

Presumably rogue states already know that using nuclear weapons against U.S. interests could trigger U.S. nuclear retaliation. However, they may view biological weapons as more usable, more credible, and less risky, not to mention easier to obtain or make. A U.S. pledge not to use nuclear weapons first would make them even more eager to acquire—and less hesitant to brandish and use—biological weapons.

While it is possible to imagine a biological attack that would not warrant a nuclear response, this is no reason to discard the option of a nuclear response against any and all possible biological attacks.

When thousands of Soviet nuclear weapons were poised to strike, the first use of nuclear weapons by the United States risked a general nuclear cataclysm. In contrast, U.S. nuclear retaliation for a biological attack by a rogue state would risk, at worst, another WMD attack—awful to be sure, but worth the risk in order to deter biological use in the first place.

More likely, having proven its resolve with a presumably selective nuclear detonation, the United States would deter further escalation and prevail. In any case, being prepared to respond to an attack by weapons of mass destruction with nuclear weapons—and by saying so—the United States would be less likely to have to do so.

Of course, U.S. nuclear retaliation for a biological attack would be a grave, world-changing event. But it would not imperil the nation and its global interests, let alone human viability. And it would make it less likely that any weapon of mass destruction—at least a biological or nuclear one—would ever be used again, and certainly not against the United States.

A fresh idea

The strongest argument for a nuclear no-first-use pledge during the Cold War was that it could have saved the United States from nuclear hell. The strongest argument against such a pledge was that it could have condemned the United States to a communist hell.

Now that the Soviet Union is gone, neither argument is persuasive. Concepts saved in the attic from a different time, a different world, are not helpful. Both nuclear first-use and nuclear no-first-use are out of date. A fresh idea is needed.

During the Cold War, the United States would not exclude a nuclear response to any aggression. It was motivated by both a general concern, the Soviet menace, and a specific concern, a tank attack on West Germany. The former was the context and the latter was the sharp focal point of U.S. first-use doctrine. It was surely the specific prospect that the United States might resort to nuclear weapons if war broke out in Europe that got the Kremlin's attention.

Now, the United States wants rogue states to think that the use of biological weapons could cause a disproportionate response; it wants them to feel this fear quite sharply. To the extent that the United States fails to pinpoint this in defining the purpose of nuclear weapons, that fear will be dull and its utility will be lost.

Current U.S. policy regarding the use of nuclear weapons is not substantially different from its general Cold War policy. The United States maintains ambiguity about the circumstances under which it would resort to nuclear weapons. Despite growing and enduring U.S. conventional military superiority, even a nuclear response to conventional attack is not excluded.

Being prepared to respond to an attack by weapons of mass destruction with nuclear weapons—and by saying so—the United States would be less likely to have to do so.

And yet, so unreal is the thought that the United States would use nuclear weapons in response to conventional attack that the current open-ended policy actually dulls deterrence. As long as the United States refuses to rule out an option that is now patently incredible (nuclear retaliation for conventional aggression), it undermines the credibility of an option that could prove crucial (nuclear retaliation for biological attack). Ambiguity is sometimes useful. But in the new era, it does more harm than good.

The United States should explicitly warn that it might respond with a weapon of mass destruction—nuclear weapons—to an attack by a weapon of mass destruction against U.S. interests. (Chemical weapons could be included, although it could be made clear that the greater concern is biological weapons.)

But that is not enough. To sharpen the fear to a finer point, the United States should also say that it foresees no need to use nuclear weapons except in response to attacks by weapons of mass destruction.

A declaratory policy along these lines would reinforce deterrence by erasing the incredible aspect of current policy—that is, nuclear response to conventional aggression. And it would bolster the taboo against first use of any weapon of mass destruction—a taboo that today appears too weak for comfort.

In past efforts to stem the spread of nuclear weapons, the United States has said, in effect, that it would not use nuclear weapons against states that forswear them. But what if a state acquired biological weapons, which can kill Americans no less effectively than nuclear explosives? What if the state used them?

In light of this danger, the United States should retract its pledge not to use nuclear weapons against any non-nuclear states. If a non-nuclear state used a biological weapon against the United States, it should be on notice that it could pay a heavy nuclear price.

The United States wants rogue states to think that the use of biological weapons could cause a disproportionate response; it wants them to feel this fear quite sharply.

How would a U.S. policy of no-first-WMD-use work toward another nuclear power, say, Russia or China? Now that Russia's conventional forces are weak, it has reversed its doctrine not to use nuclear weapons first. Given its decaying command-and-control system and the possibility of political turmoil, this shift could prove dangerous.

Further, Russia seems to be maintaining its ability to assemble and use biological weapons. An American policy not to be the first to use a weapon of mass destruction would delegitimize Russia's growing reliance on nuclear weapons and sharpen deterrence against its use of biological weapons. Perhaps a U.S. no-first-WMD-use pledge could be used to goad Russia into a similar policy, which would be a great relief. As for China— which has said in every available forum that it would never be the first to use nuclear weapons—it would likely applaud and might even subscribe to such a U.S. pledge.

One hopes the time will come when nuclear weapons can be retired. With its natural and durable advantages, the United States should want this as much as any country. Nuclear weapons may be hard to outlaw, but the world may eventually outlive or outgrow the nuclear era. Perhaps the information age, with its emphasis on precision weapons, can reduce the scale of deadly conflict. If, as well, the new age blesses free-market democracies with superior power, the world may become increasingly safe and the need to rely on nuclear weapons to keep it safe may fade away.

We are not there yet. Rogue states are on the ropes, but they can hang on and do great harm if they acquire weapons of mass destruction. By concentrating nuclear deterrence on this particular problem, by creating a sharp fear, and by limiting the purpose of nuclear weapons to retaliation for attacks by weapons of mass destruction, the United States may help move the world a step closer to a world in which none of these horrible weapons would ever again be used.

The debate about nuclear use is a reasoned one among reasonable people. The argument for complete ambiguity is understandable, especially when coming from officials conditioned to hedge against all possibilities. However, in this case, ambiguity weakens credibility and dulls deterrence.

By limiting the purpose of nuclear weapons to retaliation for attacks by weapons of mass destruction, the United States may help move the world a step closer to a world in which none of these horrible weapons would ever again be used.

Similarly, renewed interest in having the United States give up completely the option to use nuclear weapons first is understandable, what with the dramatic turn of events since 1989. However, nuclear no-first-use is as much a Cold War concept as official nuclear declaratory policy is. It was motivated by a fear of nuclear Armageddon, compared to which the future potential of biological war was hardly noticed.

Just because U.S. official nuclear first-use policy is now obsolete, it does not mean that the time is right for its Cold War antithesis. The aim, after all, is to spare humanity from the horror of mass destruction, whatever the technology of causing it.

10

The Chemical Weapons Convention Is Unenforceable

Frank J. Gaffney Jr.

Frank J. Gaffney Jr. held senior positions in the Department of Defense under President Ronald Reagan. He is currently the Director of the Center for Security Policy in Washington, D.C. He was aided in the preparation of this document by Douglas J. Feith, a member of the Center's board of advisers, and Tryfan Evans, an associate at the Center.

Ratified by the U.S. Senate in 1997 after years of debate, the Chemical Weapons Convention treaty (CWC) is a hollow piece of international legislation that contains no effective measures for banning chemical weapons. Because the manufacture of chemical weapons is fairly easy to conceal, locating such factories would be difficult with or without a treaty. Even if inspectors working under treaty authority did find compelling evidence that a nation was building chemical weapons, it is unlikely that an international community—made up of many nations that are antagonistic toward America—would band together to support the United States in calling for sanctions against the violator. Furthermore, the CWC could be turned against the U.S., permitting unfriendly governments to request inspection of U.S. chemical plants and gain access to guarded information that could be used to further foreign chemical weapons programs. A new call to broaden the scope of the antiquated and unenforceable Biological Weapons Convention (BWC) of 1972 is equally misguided. The only ways to counter chemical and biological weapons are to curb the dissemination of the technologies to construct such weapons and to maintain a formidable threat or display of military force.

On August 20 [1998], the Clinton administration launched cruise missiles at the Sudanese capital of Khartoum. The purpose of the attack was to destroy an industrial facility believed to be involved in the production of Empta, a chemical compound whose only known use is as a precursor for the deadly VX nerve agent.

The attack, which has generated its share of controversy, has had at least one welcome effect. In the process of removing the Al-Shifa plant from the map, it put squarely on the map the issue of the proliferation of chemical and biological weapons (CBW). But the strike also demonstrated the difficulty of attempting to slow, to say nothing of ending, this threat to the security of the United States and its allies—a threat becoming more and more grave by the hour.

Uses of chemical weapons

Chemical weapons (CW) pose several distinct dangers.[1] First, they can be used in combat to inflict tremendous casualties and shift the "correlation of forces." This is especially true when they are employed against forces unprepared, ill-equipped, and/or untrained in chemical warfare. Using a nerve agent and mustard gas, for example, Saddam Hussein's army in the Iran-Iraq war was able to shatter the "human-wave" attacks upon which the numerically superior Iranians pinned their hopes for victory.

But chemical weapons are useful even against forces prepared for them. Detonated over sites where tanks, infantry-fighting vehicles, ammunition, and other equipment are stored, or over military airfields, ports, and other facilities, persistent chemical agents (as opposed to those that readily dissipate) can be valuable in disrupting or even preventing mobilization. Such attacks could be particularly effective against a country like Israel whose defense relies upon the rapid response of its reserve units.

Finally, as a weapon of war, chemical attacks can seriously degrade the advantage that would otherwise accrue to armed forces equipped with high-technology weaponry. Typically, such systems require effective eye-hand coordination and unobstructed vision. By forcing soldiers into protective suits that inevitably interfere with performance, an attacker can severely compromise the qualitative edge that countries like the United States (and Israel) depend upon.

As successive American governments recognized . . . it is exceedingly difficult to distinguish between facilities producing a range of legitimate chemical products for civilian use . . . and those producing chemical weapons.

Aside from their use in war, chemical weapons are also instruments of terror. A number of states have demonstrated a willingness to employ such weapons against undefended populations to achieve strategic objectives. The Soviet Union did so as part of its effort to suppress the Afghan resistance, and so did Saddam Hussein against ethnic Kurds in northern

---

1. In what follows I shall be focusing primarily on chemical weapons. In general, however, everything that can be said of them can be said of biological weapons as well—in spades.

Iraq. Toxin weapons—chemical agents produced by biological processes—are also thought to have been used by Soviet-equipped Laotian forces against the Hmong tribes in the early 1980's. Before the Gulf War, in line with his genocidal designs against the Jewish state, Saddam announced his intention to rain chemical weapons down on Israel.

Nor is the ability to deploy chemical weapons against civilians any longer restricted to states. In 1995, the Japanese cult Aum Shim Rikyo demonstrated its capacity to manufacture, stockpile, and employ the nerve agent Sarin; fortunately, only a few people were killed (and some 5,000 injured) in attacks in Tokyo's subways that could have resulted in many times the casualties. In the case of the Al-Shifa facility in Sudan, its benefactor—and beneficiary—is said to have been Osama bin Laden, the Saudi expatriate terrorist. Whether or not this turns out to be true, it is clear that if Aum Shinrikyo was able to secure the know-how and technology to manufacture modest quantities of chemical weaponry, bin Laden and other well-financed terrorists are or will soon be able to do so as well—particularly if they can secure technical support from sources in Russia (as the Japanese sect did) or (as is no doubt the case with Sudan) from Iraq.

Proliferation of chemical weapons

Who is now equipped with CW arsenals, and is helping others acquire them?

- Russia has the largest stockpile on the planet. Although estimates vary widely, the figure cited in arms-control documents—some 40,000 agent tons—is almost certainly understated by a substantial degree. Despite strenuous Russian representations to the contrary, there is also reason to believe that the Kremlin is continuing to amass chemical weapons—including, according to defectors from the Russian CW program, new strains specifically designed to be more lethal, more effective in penetrating Western defenses, and less susceptible to antidotes. Compounding the threat posed by Russia's arsenal is the steadfast refusal of its political leadership to enforce export-control regulations against the spread of CW technology.
- China also has a sizable and active production complex, despite the fact that, like Russia, it has signed and ratified the 1993 Chemical Weapons Convention (CWC). China has also aggressively exported CW technology to other states. According to a March 1996 report in the *Washington Post,* virtually complete factories suitable for making chemical weapons have been transferred to Iran; later that same year, according to the *Washington Times,* China delivered to Iran some 400 metric tons of carbon sulfide and other chemicals used in the production of nerve agents.
- Thanks in no small measure to this assistance, Iran is today considered to have the largest CW stockpile in the third world. According to the *Proliferation Primer,* a U.S. Senate report published in January 1998, Iran—another signatory to the CWC—"fully intends to maintain a chemical-weapons capability well into the future." The country's newest ballistic missile, the Shahab-3, is believed to be capable of delivering chemical weapons against Israel and other targets throughout most of the Middle East.

- Then there is Iraq, which, despite seven years of sanctions and the most intrusive on-site inspections regime ever implemented, continues to pose a significant CW threat to U.S. forces and allies in the Gulf. In July 1997, Rolf Ekeus, then-chairman of the United Nations Special Commission (UNSCOM), warned that Iraq was still hiding chemical weapons and that "3,000 kilograms of VX" were "missing." UNSCOM's most recent six-month report notes the continuing inadequacy of procedures that are supposed to account for chemical and biological warheads and munitions capable of being outfitted with mustard gas. According to UNSCOM, approximately 46,000 chemical weapons (some of them disarmed, others battle-ready) have been retained by the Iraqi government.

- "Since the late 1980's," the *Proliferation Primer* reports, "North Korea has . . . expanded its chemical-weapons program and has placed a high priority on military and civilian chemical defense. According to the [U.S.] Department of Defense, Pyongyang is currently capable of producing large quantities of nerve, blister, and blood chemical-warfare agents." North Korea's capabilities were spelled out in a document released last year by the South Korean military. Not only has the North amassed a 1,000-ton stockpile—70 tons of which could be used immediately upon South Korean population centers—but it continues to produce 15.2 tons of chemical weapons each day; in a time of crisis, that figure could be stepped up to 40 tons per day. Given Pyongyang's willingness to sell virtually everything in its inventory, it also seems likely that North Korea will offer for sale the chemical (and, perhaps, biological) weapons that go aboard the missiles it is now making available to countries like Iran, Syria, and Pakistan.

- An August 1997 report on the Christian Broadcasting Network revealed that Syria "appears to be deploying deadly new nerve agents loaded onto missiles at sites near the cities of Hama and Homs." Other sources similarly suggest a substantial Syrian capability for delivering chemical weapons—notably, its arsenal of up to 150 Scud missiles built with the assistance of China and North Korea. The possibility cannot be ruled out that, with the Middle East's largest chemical-weapons stockpile and an eroding conventional capability, Syria may be tempted into a devastating preemptive strike on Israeli population centers.

Flaws of the Chemical Weapons Convention

Given the foregoing litany, it should be obvious that the Chemical Weapons Convention [CWC]—signed in 1993 and ratified last year [1997] after intense debate in the U.S. Senate—is not preventing the parties to it, let alone nonsignatories, from pursuing active chemical-weapons programs. And yet, until last month's attack on the Sudanese plant, this treaty has been the centerpiece of the Clinton administration's efforts to contend with the proliferation of chemical weapons. The story of this agreement offers a cautionary lesson for all those nations, the United States among them, that may be doomed to pay a heavy price for its inherent shortcomings.

For decades, the idea of banning chemical weapons had languished in the salons of multilateral arms controllers—and languished with good reason. As successive American governments recognized, and as the aftermath of the Khartoum attack bears out, it is exceedingly difficult to distinguish between facilities producing a range of legitimate chemical products for civilian use (fertilizers, pesticides, pharmaceuticals, etc.) and those producing chemical weapons. Moreover, even if a plant is engaged in the manufacture of commercial products, there is no known means of ensuring that its equipment will not shortly be put to CW-related uses. It was for precisely this reason that the United States properly declined when in the early 1990's Libya's Muammar Qaddafi proposed to allay our concerns about his suspected chemical-weapons facility at Rabta by offering to subject it to on-site inspection.

The CWC cannot prevent—or even ensure detection of—the covert production of chemical weapons.

There is a related consideration here. Knowingly or not, industrialized nations have fostered the spread throughout the developing world of "dual-use" infrastructures with at least the capability of producing chemical weapons. West Germany's assistance to Libya in building and outfitting its Rabta complex—supposedly for peaceful purposes only—is an infamous but hardly unique example. Exporters of chemical technology are either indifferent to the potential for misuse or willing to overlook it in the interest of making a sale.

With these facts in mind, U.S. policy-makers generally agreed that in controlling chemical weapons, the best hope lay in the Geneva Convention of 1925, which prohibited their first use—a relatively verifiable if not currently enforceable restraint. But in 1984, then-Secretary of State George Shultz, with the active support of Vice President George Bush—the latter had made a personal cause of the campaign to outlaw chemical weapons—took it upon himself to announce that the United States would place on the table a treaty for a global ban on production, stockpiling, and use. Despite four years of negotiations that confirmed the inadvisability of a chemical-weapons convention, Bush, now campaigning to succeed Ronald Reagan, promised to be the President who would "rid the world of chemical weapons."

Once elected, Bush authorized a number of concessions designed to conclude the treaty. Among the more irresponsible were two initiatives taken after Desert Storm in 1991: that the United States would "forswear the use of chemical weapons for any reason, including retaliation in-kind with CW, against any state, effective when the [Convention] enters into force"; and that the United States would "drop its position that we must be allowed to keep 2 percent of our CW stockpile until all CW-capable states have joined the Convention." With these steps, the United States was launched on a glide-path to unilateral chemical disarmament.

Although President Bush was able to see the treaty finalized before he left office, it was left to his successor, Bill Clinton, an eager partisan of the CWC, to seek Senate approval for it late in his first term. In the fall of

1996, however, faced with virulent opposition, he withdrew the treaty rather than risk rejection. Six months later, with critical assistance from Senate Majority Leader Trent Lott, the Clinton administration succeeded at last in securing the two-thirds majority needed for ratification. Central to its success was the oft-repeated representation that the Convention was a legacy of Presidents Reagan and Bush—proof if ever there were one of how an ill-considered commitment by parties who think they are in control of events can be shamelessly exploited by later parties to legitimize the bad deal that results.

Chemical Weapons Convention has no teeth

Among the numerous claims made for the Chemical Weapons Convention in the course of the Senate debate were that it would banish poison gas; protect American troops from chemical attack; and either stop rogue nations or terrorists from building chemical weapons or give the "international community" the tools to prevent, halt, or punish those who did so. Each of these claims is spurious.

The CWC cannot prevent—or even ensure detection of—the covert production of chemical weapons. Since sites are easy to conceal, even the sorts of inspection permitted by the CWC may not "prove" illegal activities. And even if evidence is forthcoming and compelling, it is unlikely to be judged dispositive by an "international community" reluctant to support the United States in a dispute with a fraternal third-world regime. Does anyone think that a consensus supporting the U.S. position on the Sudanese plant would ever emerge from the sort of international investigation Khartoum has demanded? The same would be true of efforts to prosecute violations of the CWC by appealing to the institution created to implement it, the multilateral Organization for the Prohibition of Chemical Weapons (OPCW).

> *The Convention's data-exchange and on-site inspection requirements . . . offer a ready avenue for the unauthorized transfer of sensitive and proprietary information—in other words, industrial spying.*

A further complication arises from the fact that foreign companies are likely to be implicated in—and thus seek to excuse—suspect activity arising from the sale of dual-use technology. At a press conference in Amman on August 22 [1998], Ahmad Salem, a Jordanian engineer who asserts responsibility for putting together the construction plans for the Al-Shifa plant, claimed, probably correctly, that "some of the equipment used at the factory was supplied by Swedish, American, Danish, Belgian, and other foreign firms." He added, emphatically: "There is no chance this factory could be used to produce chemical weapons; it was designed to produce medicine for people and animals." He could be right about the character of the design, as well; but modern pharmaceutical technology can be—and often is—used for both civilian and chemical-weapons-related production.

Opening the doors to industrial spies

What is more, far from inhibiting the proliferation of chemical weapons, the CWC will assuredly exacerbate it. The Convention's data-exchange and on-site inspection requirements, for example, offer a ready avenue for the unauthorized transfer of sensitive and proprietary information—in other words, industrial spying. Such espionage by foreign governments and enterprises is already a serious problem, and U.S. chemical companies, as world leaders in their industry, are an especially attractive target. In testimony before the Senate in May 1997, Bruce Merrifield, a former Under Secretary of Commerce who has considerable experience with the chemical industry, asserted that access provided under the CWC would permit a trained engineer or chemist from a foreign country to identify a company's trade secrets even without actually entering its facilities.

Training . . . to equip inspectors to ferret out covert [biological weapons] programs may wind up teaching foreign nationals how to defeat such inspections in their own countries.

Similar concerns are now being voiced, ironically enough, by the Chemical Manufacturers Association (CMA), one of the most outspoken original proponents of the CWC. During the Senate debate, the CMA insisted that "routine inspection of chemical facilities can quickly and efficiently verify compliance, . . . with little or no disruption in production activities." But a CMA report published in August 1997 under the title Economic Espionage: The Looting of America's Economic Security in the Information Age takes a more realistic view, citing the ease with which foreign operatives can obtain confidential information using techniques that "range from 'dumpster diving' or 'trash trawling' . . . to elaborate multifaceted efforts including high-surveillance and other information-collection methods."

A threat of a different nature lies in the extraordinary opportunity for mischief-making against the U.S. and its allies afforded by the regime of on-site inspections. Inspectors from governments unfriendly to the West are likely to find "evidence" of illegal chemical production and stockpiling even where none exists. This will be an especially grave problem for Israel if the Netanyahu government makes the mistake of ratifying the CWC, which its predecessor signed in January 1993.

No less troubling is the other side of this particular coin: training offered by the OPCW to equip inspectors to ferret out covert programs may wind up teaching foreign nationals how to defeat such inspections in their own countries. David Kay, one of UNSCOM's former chief inspectors, recalls an Iraqi official's delight in telling how he had used his experience as an inspector for the International Atomic Energy Agency to conceal Saddam Hussein's aggressive pursuit of nuclear arms in violation of the Nuclear Nonproliferation Treaty (NPT).

Saddam was able to engage in this sort of deception as a result of the NPT's "Atoms for Peace" program. But the CWC contains, in Article XI, its own version of this program, derisively dubbed "Poisons for Peace" by former Under Secretary of Defense Fred Iklé. In obliging member nations to cooperate in the field of chemical activities "for purposes not prohibited under this Convention," it creates a cover for trade that contributes to the proliferation it is supposed to ban.

According to the OPCW's deputy director John Gee, there are already huge discrepancies in reports concerning the transfer of chemicals that could be used to manufacture weapons or adapted to serve that purpose. Even more glaring is the collaboration between China and Iran on a factory making glass-lined equipment that, as the *Washington Times* noted last October, is "essential in the production of chemical-warfare agent precursors." Since the factory is a "dual-use" facility, China and Iran, both of which have ratified the CWC, are able to contend that what they are doing is not only legal but, in light of the Convention's Article XI, wholly unobjectionable.

In short, the CWC is inherently unverifiable and fatally inadequate to the job of detecting or proving the existence of covert activity. Anyone doubting this need look no further than Saddam Hussein's success in defeating the vastly more intrusive, timely, and comprehensive inspections that have, until recently, been conducted in Iraq to find and destroy prohibited weapons of mass destruction and ballistic missiles. At the same time, the CWC openly enhances the opportunities for signatories to acquire the very weapons the CWC ostensibly exists to deny them.

Updating the faulty Biological Weapons Convention

The fact that the Chemical Weapons Convention is unverifiable and counterproductive, however, has not stopped President Clinton and other arms-control enthusiasts from issuing a call to "update," along the same lines, a 1972 convention covering biological weapons.

As I noted at the outset, biological weapons (BW) have much in common with chemical weapons. Both, thanks to their potential for mass destruction and the ease with which they can be produced and stockpiled, are the "poor man's atom bomb." But biological weapons are also significantly simpler to produce than chemical weapons—and if the objective is to sow terror and indiscriminate destruction, far more efficient.

The horrific threat posed by the deliberate dissemination of [biological] substances has not been mitigated by the 1972 Biological Weapons Convention (BWC), which, unlike the CWC, makes no pretense of verifiably banning production or stockpiling.

For these reasons, Russia, China, and virtually every rogue state are believed to harbor active BW programs centering on naturally occurring or genetically altered strains of such terrifying diseases as anthrax, botulism, plague, and smallpox. Some have gone so far as to "weaponize" these viruses. Worse yet, Russia and Iraq are said to have experimented with "cocktails" combining more than one virus to maximize a weapon's lethality and complicate defensive measures against it.

The horrific threat posed by the deliberate dissemination of such substances has not been mitigated by the 1972 Biological Weapons Convention (BWC), which, unlike the CWC, makes no pretense of verifiably banning production or stockpiling. It is, rather, a gentleman's agreement, an international declaration of good intentions without means of assuring the detection or punishment of violations. Hence the Clinton administration's proposal to add provisions modeled after those of the CWC.

That proposal is seriously misguided. Should the negotiations now under way with other countries bear fruit, the effect will be even more contrary to American and Western interests than in the case of the CWC. As Alan P. Zelicoff, a scientist at Sandia National Laboratory and a technical adviser to the U.S. delegation to the BWC negotiations, warned in a letter to the *Washington Post* last January:

> Facilities engaged in legitimate activities can be incorrectly assessed to be in violation of the Convention. Conversely, sites that are demonstrably in compliance with the Convention easily can convert to illicit activity within hours after the departure of inspectors. . . . In just a few days or weeks, biological weapons can be manufactured in militarily significant quantities in a site no larger than a small house.

Moreover, the U.S. biotech industry is at least as vulnerable as the chemical industry to pilfering and other forms of espionage, and the consequences of technology transfers (both legitimate and illegal) are likely to be vastly more damaging. One can only hope, therefore, that cooler heads like Zelicoff's will prevail. For, as he concluded his letter, "While biological-weapons proliferation is a serious security threat . . . , it is all too easy to make this terrible problem even worse with feckless measures."

The right solutions

If agreements like the Chemical Weapons Convention are not the answer, are other options likely to prove more practical? The short answer is yes, although none of them, alone or in combination with others, can promise an end to the danger.

- Multilateral agreements among nations with advanced chemical and biotech industries can be helpful in curbing the transfer of technology, supplies, and know-how to rogue states and their sponsors. In the past, an informal consortium known as the Australia Group has been able to shame member nations into better behavior. The utility of this sort of arrangement, however, is considerably reduced when the technology in question becomes widely available—which, thanks in some degree to the CWC itself, is fast becoming the case. This alone shows the folly of treaties that facilitate the movement of dual-capable equipment.
- The actual threat posed by proliferation may be met in part by strict enforcement of the 1925 Geneva Convention. This accord, prohibiting the first use of chemical weapons, is relatively easy to verify; were mechanisms in place to ensure that violators faced real and

substantial costs, some CW attacks might thereby be prevented.

- The American cruise-missile attack on the Al-Shifa plant illustrates another option: the physical destruction of facilities suspected of involvement in chemical or biological weapons. This, in the final analysis, may be the only sure means of putting them out of business. But it has certain drawbacks as well. For one thing, it is not always easy to ensure that the right facility is in the cross-hairs. Then, too, attacks on others' sovereign territory cannot be undertaken lightly—certainly not too frequently in peacetime and perhaps, depending upon the target country's capacity for lethal retribution, not at all. It is a tricky business to blow up CBW sites located in, or upwind from, populated areas—the locales favored by unscrupulous dictators for just that reason. Finally, in the wake of the American strikes, the already evident trend toward hardening and concealing weapons-production complexes underground is likely to accelerate.
- The limitations of both diplomacy and direct action bring us at last to the issue of deterrence. A formidable military posture—and the perceived will to use it—can cause some potential adversaries to think twice about initiating the use of chemical weapons. Others may be more influenced by a credible threat of thermonuclear retaliation. After the Gulf war, Iraqi officials let it be known that the possibility of a U.S. nuclear strike dissuaded Saddam from using whatever chemical and/or biological weapons he had on hand.

Would the United States really be willing to exercise its nuclear option in such circumstances? Concern that it would not has prompted some to urge that we be sure to retain a modest stockpile of binary chemical weapons (i.e., munitions composed of two relatively innocuous chemicals that combine to form a toxic agent only after being fired). Others, who believe the U.S. does not need a CW arsenal at this time, agree that we should not be precluded by dint of treaty obligations from acquiring one in the future.

It is a scandal that the United States does not already have the means to protect its people as well as its troops and allies against the systems that deliver chemical and biological weapons.

In any event, Western nations are well-advised to develop and deploy means of protecting their forces and citizens against the effects of CBW attack, and the sooner the better. A realistic program would go well beyond training and equipping "first responders"—emergency, medical, and law-enforcement personnel—to include significantly improved intelligence to warn against the sources and timing of attacks; extensive planning for the relocation and treatment of those exposed; the production and stockpiling of antibiotics and other medications; and measures to ensure the safety of the nation's food supply against biological assault.

Above all, it is a scandal that the United States does not already have the means to protect its people as well as its troops and allies against the systems that deliver chemical and biological weapons. Our single biggest vulnerability in this connection is our inability to shoot down even a single ballistic missile aimed at our territory. This situation can be most readily remedied by modifying the Navy's AEGIS air-defense system to enable it to intercept incoming missiles. But the Clinton administration, in deference to the 1972 ABM treaty, has refused to allow the existing infrastructure to be used for that critical purpose.

One way or another, chemical and biological threats almost certainly lurk in our future. Arms-control agreements, which anyway do not address but rather exacerbate the problem, are no substitute for the much more urgent task before us: to take the lead in dissuading those who may be contemplating such threats, to disable their capacity to carry them out, and—if all else fails—to make sure that we, our armed forces, and our allies are defended against them. As in so many other critical areas of foreign policy, what is required is realism and leadership—exactly the two qualities that are now in perilously short supply.

11

Local Governments' Responses to Biological and Chemical Terrorism

Karen Ann Coburn

Karen Ann Coburn has written several articles of local and national interest for Governing *magazine.*

Although local emergency response authorities have often felt ill-informed by the federal government regarding the potential dangers of terrorist attacks, in recent years the lines of communication have been better established. In the wake of the 1995 Oklahoma City bombing (in which the Alfred P. Murrah Federal Building was destroyed by convicted terrorist Timothy McVeigh), President Bill Clinton created new protocols outlining how local and federal authorities should be coordinated to respond to attacks on American soil. Furthermore, federal authorities have been sharing more information regarding potential threats with local response teams and have been offering training to local officials on new technologies and other countermeasures meant to deter or deal with chemical or biological attacks. It is now up to local governments to determine what equipment and training they will need—and can afford—to contend with the potential threats to their communities.

For $3,000 a pop, any city concerned about the threat of terrorism can equip its emergency response personnel with high-tech, gas-proof anti-contamination suits. The puffy, space-age outfits are sure to provide a sense of security in the face of a nuclear, chemical or biological incident.

Those with more limited budgets might opt for "turnout bags." At roughly $200 each, a turnout bag contains a lightweight disposable suit, booties and gloves made of a plastic-wrap material named Saranek over another durable plastic product called Tyvek. It also comes with a mask that has a special filter for biological and chemical agents, as well as a skin decontamination kit.

Before 1995, only a handful of public safety directors in this country contemplated either choice. But the bombing of the Alfred P. Murrah Federal Building in Oklahoma City made clear that terrorists—foreign or domestic—can strike in the nation's heartland as well as in international centers such as New York City. Another consequence of that tragedy was to spur the federal government to begin sharing its vast knowledge of weapons of mass destruction with those that may need it most—local governments.

Lack of cooperation in the past

In the past, federal actions bred suspicion among local officials. Indeed, until quite recently, many emergency workers felt like canaries in a coal mine. That's because federal plans for domestic terrorism always presumed that the first responders on the scene would be killed or seriously injured, says Kathleen Henning, emergency management coordinator for Montgomery County, Maryland. Some federal training exercises, for instance, refer to the blistering and death of first responders as a way for authorities to confirm that chemical weapons have been used. For the police officers, fire fighters and emergency medical technicians who must wait several hours on the scene before federal authorities arrive, that approach was clearly disturbing.

And before James Lee Witt took over the Federal Emergency Management Agency (FEMA) in 1992, the perception among local governments was that information traveled in only one direction: from the top down. Other federal agencies, such as the Department of Defense and the FBI, continue to have a poor reputation in their dealings with the local emergency response community. Montgomery County's Henning adds, "For a long time, you would call up federal people" with questions on terrorism "and they would say, 'We can't share that information with you.'"

> *The bombing of the Alfred P. Murrah Federal Building in Oklahoma City made clear that terrorists—foreign or domestic—can strike in the nation's heartland as well as in international centers such as New York City.*

One thing everyone seems to agree on, though, is that public health and safety are the responsibility of the local governments. Federal officials become involved in the aftermath of a disaster for two reasons: The FBI comes in to investigate whether a federal crime has been committed; and the Federal Emergency Management Agency [FEMA], the armed services and a panoply of other federal agencies may be called upon to provide support in the form of expertise, personnel and equipment. State governments also back local responders with hazardous materials teams and National Guard units, coordinate resources from other localities and act as a liaison between the locals and the feds in the early stages of an incident. In addition, officials at the state level hold the purse strings on federal emergency preparedness funding.

While the roles appear clear-cut, the lines of communication usually are not. A local government does not request federal help directly. Instead, a designated state liaison calls the FBI or FEMA. If terrorism is suspected, Presidential Directive 39 goes into effect. Introduced shortly after the Oklahoma City bombing, PD 39 outlines, for the first time, a specific plan for intergovernmental coordination during a terrorist incident. Even with the new protocol, FEMA spokesman Phil Cogan says, "We're probably going to learn about it from CNN." Indeed, the response to each terrorist event is unique. "There may be lag time, or no lag time at all," Cogan says, adding that there are "as many scenarios as you can imagine."

Nunn-Lugar: A critical first step

Even more recently, the federal Anti-Terrorism and Effective Death Penalty Act authorized the Department of Justice to offer training to localities through FEMA's National Fire Academy. In addition, the 1996 Defense Against Weapons of Mass Destruction Act (also known as Nunn-Lugar, after its primary U.S. Senate sponsors) offers the biggest step yet in preparing local response teams.

Funded through the Department of Defense and coordinated by FEMA, Nunn-Lugar provides an unprecedented $160 million to train the 120 largest communities over the next five years. So far, teams of representatives from six federal agencies—the Defense Department, FEMA, the FBI, the Health and Human Services Department, the Environmental Protection Agency and the Energy Department—have traveled to seven cities. The teams are teaching local forces how to deal with explosives, as well as nuclear, chemical and biological attacks.

Officials in Harrisonburg, Virginia, know that the threat of weapons of mass destruction is quite real. In 1996, the police department in the Shenandoah Valley town of 33,000 was contacted by authorities in Nashville, who believed that a Harrisonburg doctor was illegally manufacturing chemical and biological weapons for use in Tennessee.

With the help of the fire department's hazardous materials team, as well as chemists from James Madison University and the local branch of Merck pharmaceuticals, Harrisonburg police searched the doctor's home and retrieved a variety of lethal chemicals, including Ricin, a toxin derived from castor beans. With their role in the investigation over—the federal case against the doctor is being tried in Nashville—local officials were only too glad to hand the deadly substances over to the FBI.

Federal agencies, such as the Department of Defense and FBI, continue to have a poor reputation in their dealings with the local emergency response community.

Because Harrisonburg's fire department had a well-trained "hazmat" team and a working relationship with local chemists, it was confident of its ability to handle a chemical or biological threat. Indeed, a 1996 study by the National Governors' Association (NGA) confirms that access to a hazmat team, whether run locally or by the state, is an integral part of any anti-terrorism plan. Chemical agents—such as the nerve gas sarin that was manufactured by a religious cult and released in Tokyo's subway system in 1995—are easily and cheaply manufactured. Hazmat teams, already adept at handling a variety of dangerous chemicals, can be trained to detect and identify the most deadly varieties.

The NGA study also found that states with nuclear reactors already have plans to deal with a radioactive release. State and local authorities report that they are least prepared to deal with an attack of biological agents, which could cause deadly outbreaks of anthrax, bubonic plague and salmonella. If cultured properly, these diseases can be spread in numerous ways. They are difficult and sometimes impossible to detect.

Training for potential emergencies

Under Nunn-Lugar, meetings with locals include a comprehensive self-assessment to determine what each city perceives as its particular training needs. Training is then specialized to fit that city. Phoenix, for instance, chose to expand its training to include first responders in neighboring communities. Technical experts from the Department of Defense and other agencies will return to provide classroom training and practical exercises focusing on chemical and biological incidents for a select group of emergency responders. Incident commanders, those officials selected to coordinate local response, learn how to treat large numbers of casualties and develop plans for chemical and biological incidents.

Nunn-Lugar provides an unprecedented $160 million to train the 120 largest communities [in responding to biological and chemical terrorism] over the next five years.

Phoenix, like several large cities that began training [in 1998], was no stranger to terrorism. As the first assisting emergency management team after the Oklahoma City bombing, Phoenix's emergency response community saw for itself the devastation and quickly learned the importance of minimizing the destruction of evidence.

A few months later, an Amtrak train derailment in Arizona, which killed one person and injured more than 100, was also classified as a terrorist act. Although the derailment occurred in a remote desert area outside of its jurisdiction, the Phoenix fire department was called in to help the private local fire company, which was ill-equipped for a disaster of that magnitude.

Working on the scene for about 18 hours, Phoenix officials became acutely aware of the flaws in their emergency response plan. Communications between the different responding departments was poor, largely because they were operating on different radio frequencies. Hospitals in the area were not part of an organized response plan and had trouble dealing with the deluge of patients. According to Phoenix Deputy Fire

Chief Harry Beck, the crisis ultimately "loosened a logjam" in the system that now makes it easier to work and communicate regardless of jurisdictional boundaries.

Although training meets a critical need on the local level, it may still leave rescuers exposed to deadly chemicals. Little money is available at either the state or federal levels for specialized equipment to deal with victims of nuclear, biological or chemical agents. In 1997, FEMA provided $2.5 million to localities to equip and train local firefighters. [In 1998], the Department of Justice is expected to release some of its $5 million grant to states for anti-terrorism equipment. To fill the gap for now, the Defense Department is leaving behind training kits in the Nunn-Lugar cities.

Assessing the needs of the community

Other localities should not panic, says Brett Burdick, terrorism project manager for Virginia. Instead, they should carefully evaluate their needs and capabilities. Burdick advises most localities against purchasing high-tech decontamination suits, which are designed for cleaning up the aftermath of a chemical or biological release. The first things to be concerned about when dealing with terrorism, he notes, are the same as in any hazardous materials operation: recognize, report and retreat. And for those activities, the more affordable turnout bag will suffice. Ideally, police officers, fire fighters and EMTs will each have such a bag to protect against initial vapors and splashes of chemical and biological contaminants.

Not surprisingly, though, turnout bags are a lower priority than, say, a new fire truck or police cruiser in many places. And given that a terrorist act can equate to a category 5 hurricane or a magnitude 9 earthquake, the simple truth is that few communities can really be prepared for such a cataclysmic event. Still, for those local officials concerned about their vulnerability to acts of terrorism, there are a growing number of resources. A help line (800-368-6498) for first responders now provides answers on a range of topics involving weapons of mass destruction. A separate hotline has been set up for emergency use by roughly 150 state and federal officials. If a suspected terrorist incident occurs, hotline callers will be linked directly to the National Response Center, the Department of Energy or the Army Medical Research and Material Command, and the appropriate federal authorities will be dispatched. Both phone lines will be supported by a massive database with relevant information from most federal agencies. The general public will also be able to find information on safety precautions, equipment and weapons of mass destruction on a new Internet home page.

If Nunn-Lugar can deliver on the streamlined approach it promises, local responders will not have to waste valuable time deciding whom to call. But federal contributions to training and equipment barely scratch the surface. "The rest is going to have to come out of the taxpayer base," laments Alan Caldwell, director of government relations for the International Association of Fire Chiefs. "That is, if the taxpayers think Wichita, Kansas, is a terrorist target."

12

Unearthing the Truth

John Barry

John Barry is the national security correspondent for Newsweek. *He has written or co-authored five books, his current project being a history of NATO nuclear policy. Barry has also made several television documentaries, including a six-part series on the history of NATO for the BBC.*

Although Saddam Hussein admitted that Iraq had built biological warheads, he claimed that in accordance with the mandates of the UN in the aftermath of the Gulf War these weapons had been destroyed. UN weapons inspectors in Iraq have always been dubious of Hussein's claims, and with the help of aerial photographs, a team of UN inspectors indeed located a part of the remaining stockpile of Iraqi biological weapons in Al Nibai. The find was particularly important to the UN teams because they had been accused of wasting time, money, and effort chasing phantom weapons that Hussein had already declared destroyed.

Dick Spertzel knew his trap would work. In December 1996 the leader of a United Nations Special Commission (UNSCOM) team hunting for Iraq's hidden biological weapons went on what looked like a routine inspection. Saddam Hussein had finally admitted to making bio-filled warheads, but claimed through Iraqi officials that he'd ordered them all destroyed back in 1991. The inspectors were even told where to look for the evidence: Al Nibai, a forlorn desert outpost 100 miles northwest of Baghdad. Spertzel suspected Saddam was lying, and had a plan to prove it.

Spertzel's convoy of Land Rovers headed into the desert. At Al Nibai, they found the two vast pits the Iraqis had described, and Spertzel drove his truck right down into one. The team dug for traces of destroyed warheads, then turned around and headed back to Baghdad. The digging had largely been for show. The real action was taking place 60,000 feet up. An American U-2 spy plane was passing overhead, snapping pictures of the scene—using the Land Rovers as a bull's-eye to mark the spot. Back in Washington, the photos were compared with the daily U.S. satellite shots of Iraq from July 9, 1991, the date Iraq said the warheads had been destroyed. The verdict: no one had been near the area at that time. They'd caught Saddam cold. "Allah smiles on us," Spertzel quipped to his colleagues.

The Al Nibai mission was a triumph for the beleaguered U.N. inspectors. Once dismissed as alarmists chasing a threat that didn't exist, the bioweapons crew was tenacious in its pursuit. For seven years, working from scant clues, intuition and just plain luck, it assembled irrefutable evidence that Saddam built—and still has—a formidable arsenal of biological weapons. By last November Saddam was so worried about evidence amassed by UNSCOM that he threw the inspectors out of the country, setting the stage for the current crisis. "Iraq has run out of answers, and now they're cornered," says one senior U.N. official. "Saddam's only recourse was to try to shut down UNSCOM."

In the first few years after the gulf war, he came pretty close. Ignoring intelligence reports of a possible Iraqi bioweapons program, the U.N. Security Council pressured the newly created UNSCOM to concentrate on the better-known chemical and missile stockpiles. Bioweapons were shunted to the sidelines. A small group of skeptical UNSCOM investigators, led by a British bio-expert named David Kelly, decided to take up the hunt on its own.

There wasn't much to go on. Iraq's spokeswoman on the subject, Dr. Rahib Taha—dubbed "Dr. Death" by the Western press—insisted the small amount of bioresearch Iraq had done was purely defensive. Two years passed before the team got its first break.

Working from scant clues, intuition and just plain luck, [the U.N. inspection team] assembled irrefutable evidence that Saddam built—and still has—a formidable arsenal of biological weapons.

Luckily, it was a big one. If the Iraqis had made bioweapons, Kelly figured, they would have needed highly technical equipment—things like fermenters, spray dryers and centrifuges. Kelly and Annick Paul-Henriot, a workaholic French lawyer who signed on to the bio-team, asked Iraq for a list of places where those machines could be found. To their surprise, on the last day of 1993, the Iraqis came back with a blizzard of paper detailing 23 facilities that had the equipment. It was a revelation. Why was Iraq so eager to comply? For months, the French and Russians had quietly assured Saddam that if he turned over the information, they could convince the United Nations to grant him a clean bill of health on biological weapons, and the inspectors would be off his back.

In fact, they were just getting started. Swamped with the new information, the team asked the U.S. government for help. The Pentagon turned to Spertzel, an ex-Army colonel. A microbiologist, Spertzel had worked on the United States' own biological-weapons program in the 1960s. He knew the subject cold. For five weeks he spent 13-hour days in a cubicle on the 30th floor of the U.N. building, poring over documents. His conclusion: "Iraq was hiding a biological-weapons program," he told *Newsweek*. "Nothing else made sense."

Now he had to convince his reluctant U.N. boss. UNSCOM chief Rolf Ekeus wasn't eager to admit Saddam had duped his team. But Spertzel and Paul-Henriot harassed Ekeus until he agreed to hear their pitch. They explained the Iraqis had unwittingly led UNSCOM to the program's main production plant—a desert factory at Al Hakam, 40 miles west of Baghdad. Convinced, Ekeus agreed to begin a full-scale bioweapons investigation.

Spertzel headed for Al Hakam. He couldn't believe what he saw: rows of giant fermenting tanks used to grow bioagents. This was hardly the "chicken feed" factory the Iraqis claimed.

Back in New York, Paul-Henriot was making another big discovery. If the Iraqis were growing toxic agents, they would also need plenty of bio-logical-growth medium, or BGM, as food. She sent letters to manufacturers around the world, asking if Saddam was a customer. She also sent requests to makers of fermenters and other bio-equipment.

The inspectors' deadly haul

Since 1991, U.N. inspectors have destroyed several tons of Iraqi weapons. But they believe Saddam retains a small number of Scud missiles and a stash of chemical and biological weapons.

WEAPONS DESTROYED

Chemical weapons	
Liquid precursors*	1.8 million liters
Solid precursors*	1 million kg.
Agents (sarin, mustard and VX)	480,000 liters
Chemical/biological delivery systems	
Missile warheads	30
Chemical munitions	Nearly 40,000
(including rockets, artillery and aerial bombs)	
Ballistic missiles	
Soviet-supplied Scud missiles	817
Iraqi-produced Scud warheads	15

* ingredients used to make agents such as mustard gas and sarin.

Source: National Security Council.

Several companies sent back copies of sales orders, complete with the names of the Iraqi clerks who'd signed for the shipments. Nearly all had gone through the Technical and Scientific Materials Division, or TSMD, of Iraq's Ministry of Trade—a government office the investigators had never heard of. Looking for an explanation, the team interviewed the clerks named on the sales orders. Unwittingly, two of them proudly explained that TSMD was really a division of the Iraqi military. A few months later, in January 1995, the team hit another jackpot: two European companies said they'd sold the same Iraqi agency growth medium—a staggering 39 tons of it.

The new discoveries changed everything. That January, Ekeus presented Iraqi Foreign Minister Tariq Aziz with the evidence. Over the next eight months, the Iraqi denials began to unravel. Aziz claimed the growth medium was used only in hospitals. Ekeus pressed to see it. So sorry, came the reply, it had been destroyed in riots after the gulf war. Another set of records had been destroyed in a mysterious fire that attacked a single file-cabinet drawer. Others had "fallen off the back of a truck."

Ekeus had heard enough. In April 1995 he laid out the saga before the U.N. Security Council. Saddam gave in. Though he still denied having warheads, he admitted to making 500,000 liters of anthrax and botulinum toxin, hoping his admission would satisfy his allies on the Security Council.

Spertzel headed for Al Hakam. He couldn't believe what he saw: rows of giant fermenting tanks used to grow bioagents. This was hardly the "chicken feed" factory the Iraqis claimed.

It might have, if his son-in-law hadn't blown everything. In August 1995 Gen. Hussein Kamel al-Majid—thinking Saddam was about to be overthrown—fled to Jordan. Saddam panicked, believing Kamel was telling all to the United States. He divulged key details of the bioweapons program. UNSCOM officials speculate Saddam feared Kamel would reveal Iraq had tested bioweapons on humans. After a few months, Saddam invited Kamel back home, assuring him all was forgiven. He was quickly killed.

Saddam had run out of stories. After giving away the last secrets himself, he could no longer claim his bioweapons program didn't exist. Iraq still insists the weapons were destroyed after the gulf war. But UNSCOM's new chief, Richard Butler, isn't buying. Butler is itching to get into the presidential palaces, where he believes the hidden stockpiles may be stashed. But this time, it will take more than a few Land Rovers to outfox Saddam.

13

Iraq Still Possesses a Biological and Chemical Arsenal

Bruce B. Auster and Linda Fasulo

Bruce B. Auster is a journalist for U.S. News & World Report. *Linda Fasulo is an NBC news correspondent to the United Nations.*

Despite the efforts of UN inspectors in the wake of the Gulf War, Iraq maintains chemical and biological weapon delivery systems (mainly missiles and launchers) and stockpiles of chemicals yet unaccounted for. Because biological agents are inexpensive to create, the threat of Iraq quickly rebuilding its chemical and biological arsenal is real and immediate.

Not for nothing are biological weapons called the poor man's nuclear bomb. An anthrax culture costs $45. To begin producing the organisms requires a 5-gallon fermenter, the sort used to brew beer at home. Cost: $50. Inhaling just 10,000 spores of anthrax—an amount the size of a speck of dust—is fatal.

After seven years combing Iraq for hidden weapons, inspectors for the United Nations haven't found every last fermenter in Iraq. Far from it: Stocks of Iraqi germ and gas agents, hundreds of pieces of equipment, and missiles to deliver the lethal cargo remain unaccounted for. Intelligence agencies in America and Britain believe that Iraq's past is prologue; having run an industrial-scale weapons program for years, it would take Iraq hardly any time to rebuild one if U.N. inspectors were barred. Adapting fermenters to produce seed stocks of biological warfare agents, for example, takes only a few hours.

A continuing threat

Iraq still has the expertise—and many of the ingredients—at hand for a significant chemical and biological capability:

Reprinted from "Facts and Suspicions About Iraq's Arsenal," by Bruce B. Auster and Linda Fasulo, *U.S. News & World Report*, February 23, 1998, vol. 124. Copyright ©1998 by U.S. News & World Report. Reprinted with permission. Visit us at our website www.usnews.com for additional information.

Saddam Hussein possesses tons of chemical stocks despite the efforts of the U.N. Special Commission, or UNSCOM, which has found and destroyed 127,000 gallons of chemical agents. But inspectors cannot account for 600 tons of "precursor" chemicals that could be used to manufacture a 200-ton batch of VX, a nerve gas developed by the British in the 1950s. Iraq claims to have destroyed the more than 4 tons of VX it produced before the gulf war, but the U.N. cannot confirm this. The British Foreign Office asserts that hidden Iraqi stockpiles of VX could conceivably kill everyone on the planet. The U.N. also cannot account for an additional 4,000 tons of precursor chemicals that could be used to make hundreds of tons of chemical agents less efficient than VX but still deadly.

UNSCOM knows even less about Iraq's biological weapons program, whose existence Baghdad did not acknowledge until August 1995. Iraq has since admitted producing 19,000 liters of botulinus, 8,400 liters of anthrax, and 2,000 liters of aflatoxin but claims to have destroyed it all. Chief U.N. inspector Richard Butler suspects that Iraq produced more than it has admitted, and he has told the U.N. Security Council that without monitoring, Iraq could produce enough anthrax to fill two warheads a week. Some 17 tons of growth media, in which the germs are harvested, are still unaccounted for.

Iraq still has the expertise—and many of the ingredients—at hand for a significant chemical and biological capability.

Late [in 1997], the U.N. destroyed 325 pieces of equipment from Iraq's chemical weapons program. Iraq says that nothing remains, but the U.N. cannot be sure.

Biological labs are even harder to track. The U.N. now monitors 90 sites housing 893 pieces of equipment. Unlike the sophisticated components of a nuclear weapons program, the labware needed for biological weapons research and production can be found in any college laboratory, hospital, or brewery. It is also extremely easy to conceal; the U.N. suspects Iraq has a mobile biological weapons facility.

Iraq modified its missile force to carry germ and gas warfare agents, manufacturing at least 80 such special warheads. The U.N. destroyed 30 chemical warheads but cannot be sure whether the remainder were eliminated or simply hidden. What's left of Iraq's missile force is also in dispute. The U.N. has accounted for all but two of the 819 missiles Iraq imported before the gulf war. But Iraq ran its own secret missile program, called Project 1728. Some in the intelligence community believe Iraq has hidden about two dozen missiles and mobile launchers that could be deployed on short notice. Others believe Iraq has buried key missile components, such as guidance systems and motors, which it could use to rebuild its force over time.

14

The Biological and Chemical Weapons in Iraq's Arsenal

Franklin Foer

Franklin Foer is a staff writer for U.S. News & World Report. *Previously he was on the staff of* Slate, *a Microsoft Network online news magazine.*

Iraq's biological and chemical weapons arsenal was in its infancy during the Iran-Iraq War of the 1980s. Between the conclusion of that war in 1988 and the beginning of the Persian Gulf War in 1991, Iraqi leader Saddam Hussein committed more resources to increasing the nation's stockpiles of biological and chemical weapons. In the aftermath of the Gulf War, a defeated Iraq was ordered to destroy its weapons of mass destruction. Although Iraq has stated that it has complied with the mandate, UN weapons inspection teams in Iraq have found evidence to the contrary, and Iraq has failed to provide proof that weapons yet unaccounted for have been eliminated. Among the deadly toxins Iraq is believed to still possess are VX nerve gas, the lethal anthrax bacteria, and aflatoxin, a known carcinogen. Because of Hussein's history of ruthlessly using such weapons on his enemies, concerns over his continued use of them are justified.

On one side of a hermetic glass wall in an underground chamber sit Iraqi scientists. On the other side, an Iranian prisoner of war is strapped to a bed by his arms and legs, immobilized. One of the scientists turns a valve, and a hose attached to the ceiling showers the POW with anthrax. The scientists watch the Iranian as he quickly develops a high fever and hacking cough. A day later, they observe him vomiting and breathing with difficulty. His muscles convulse. Within 36 hours, the prisoner dies. The findings from the experiment—conducted sometime during the late 1980s near a military base 50 miles south of Baghdad—are delivered to Saddam Hussein, who studies them closely and orders more tests on prisoners.

The account of these barbaric experiments comes courtesy of exiled Iraqi dissidents and anonymous Israeli intelligence officers, who leaked the reports to British newspapers. However, U.N. inspectors have had little success, and little help, corroborating these horrors. In 1994, for instance, Iraqi soldiers prevented U.N. inspectors from examining trenches thought to contain the corpses of Iranian POWs used in the experiments. The trenches, Iraq claimed, lay on a sacred ancient burial ground. Most recently, Iraq tried to exempt large tracts of land from U.N. inspection by claiming they comprise "presidential palaces."

Just what poisons might Saddam have in his chemistry set? It's impossible to know for sure, but a review of Saddam's chemical- and biological- weapons arsenal before the Gulf War probably provides the best clue.

Although Iraq has now agreed to open these sites as part of its deal to stave off U.S. air strikes, it's anyone's guess what this means in practice. And, no matter how many palaces U.N. inspectors can enter, their inspections are unlikely to make much of a difference. Over the years, Iraq's weapons program has demonstrated an implacability in the face of allied bombing and U.N. inspections that leads one to suspect the worst. But what is the worst? Just what poisons might Saddam have in his chemistry set? It's impossible to know for sure, but a review of Saddam's chemical- and biological-weapons arsenal before the Gulf War probably provides the best clue.

History of Iraq's chemical build-up

Saddam's quest for chemical and biological weapons began in earnest after the end of the Iran-Iraq war in 1988. Even though Iraq suffered catastrophic losses and came nowhere near winning a clear-cut victory, the war bolstered Saddam's ambitions. Iraq, he vowed, would become the unquestioned leader of the Arab world, as he filled the void left by the Egyptian President Gamal Abdel Nasser's death 18 years prior. In peace, the Iraqi army not only remained at full strength; it also grew to more than one million men. Iraq poured its resources into the development of chemical and biological weapons. In the months between the cease-fire with Iran and its invasion of Kuwait, Iraq expanded its cache to include 182 warheads filled with an assortment of biological weapons. During the Kuwait invasion, Saddam's forces shipped many of these warheads to air force bases and loaded them onto planes as bombs. They readied others to be launched by ballistic missiles. As best as we can tell, none was ever used.

As a condition of the Gulf War cease-fire, Iraq agreed to destroy this arsenal. And it says it has. But, of the 182 warheads Iraq admitted possessing before the war, it has provided physical evidence of the destruction of only 23. Iraq claims that the rest were destroyed during the war. But there is no evidence to verify this, because Iraqi officials refuse to hand over the paperwork supposedly supporting their contention. And even more warheads could have been produced on the sly since 1991. According to the U.N. inspectors, Iraq has as many as 16 ballistic missiles, which, in the right weather conditions, could fire warheads as far as Tel Aviv [in Israel].

Arsenal of poisons

Just what toxins could these missiles carry? At least some of the surviving warheads probably contain the nerve gas VX. Iraq admitted to producing 260 liters of it in its buildup for the Gulf War. VX is similar to sarin, the agent used by the Aum cult in their 1995 Tokyo subway attack. When as little as ten milligrams of the gas comes in contact with the skin, it is absorbed into the bloodstream. As it circulates, it destroys the enzyme acetylcholinesterase, which is essential to transmitting messages between nerves and muscles. This causes almost immediate tightness in the chest, vomiting, involuntary urination and defecation, constant erections, and unstoppable salivation. Convulsions soon become violent, and respiratory muscles cease contracting, causing death within half an hour, or in just two minutes if inhaled. VX gas could be delivered by missiles with frightening effectiveness. Upon impact, it would create an odorless, invisible cloud that would not dissipate for at least four days. Gas masks are useless against VX. Only individuals who are in sealed rooms or those who immediately inject themselves with an antidote would survive an attack.

Gas masks are useless against VX. Only individuals who are in sealed rooms or those who immediately inject themselves with an antidote would survive an attack.

Then, of course, there's anthrax—a bacterium that causes a lethal disease normally found in cattle and sheep. In the years leading up to the Gulf War, Saddam cooked up a massive 2,265 gallons of the stuff. Anthrax missiles are hardly benign. If the land where the missile hits were to absorb even some of the anthrax inside, it would be rendered uninhabitable. But, since most of the anthrax spores would be consumed in the explosion and most of what's left would have aggregated into nonlethal clumps while stored in the missile's metal casing, anthrax is less suitable than VX gas for missile delivery. Rather, the real danger posed by anthrax is its potential effectiveness in a terrorist attack. For instance, a canister of anthrax could be placed on subway tracks where it could burst open as a train rolled over it. As the train sped past, it would whip the anthrax into a cloud of deadly particles that would then spread throughout the subway system. Because anthrax is odorless and invisible, there would be no immediate sign of the attack. But, within hours, people who ingested the bacteria would begin experiencing flulike symptoms. By the time they sought treatment, the anthrax would have inflicted irreversible, fatal damage. Since bodies wouldn't pile up in the subway station, it would take investigators days to trace the cause of the deaths. Ultimately, contamination could shut down the targeted subway system for decades.

Apart from developing notorious toxins like anthrax and VX gas, Iraq has also veered into more experimental territory. For instance, Iraq is the only nation to realize the military application of aflatoxin, a carcinogenic mold that grows on dates and corn. In the lab, aflatoxin destroys the immune systems of rats. In humans, exposure to aflatoxin correlates with liver cancer. Apart from that, little is known. But in 1988 Iraq mixed aflatoxin with riot gases and loaded the mixture onto shells, which it launched against rebellious Kurdish villages. The solution purportedly caused asphyxiation and killed a large percentage of the target population. But, because it was delivered in large quantities over short distances, it was impossible to discern how much damage aflatoxin would do in a ballistic-missile attack.

And Iraq may possess other weapons. Prior to the Gulf War, Saddam's most plentiful poison was botulinum toxin, which is lethal when ingested. To be sure, scientists have doubts about how it could be effectively delivered: it would not survive inside a missile, is filtered out by the lungs when inhaled, and would probably be wiped out by decontamination processes if released into the water supply. Nonetheless, Saddam must have seen fit to produce 3,117 gallons of the stuff for some reason. There are also Israeli intelligence reports that Iraq experimented with smallpox and considered making sarin. Finally, before the Gulf War, Iraq's research was about to yield unprecedented advances in delivery systems. According to one ex-U.N. inspector, Iraqi scientists had nearly developed a remote-control plane that they could use to sprinkle anthrax over cities—a sort of crop duster of doom. Our knowledge of such efforts may not tell us exactly what Saddam is doing now, but it certainly provides ample cause for concern. After all, if Saddam gases his own citizens and orders [Nazi atrocity perpetrator Josef] Mengele-style human experiments, why would he scruple about doing even worse?

15

The U.S. Supplied Iraq with Biological and Chemical Weapons' Materials

William Blum

William Blum has been a freelance journalist in the United States, Europe, and South America. He has written extensively on U.S. involvement in foreign affairs and is the author of Killing Hope: U.S. Military and CIA Interventions Since World War II.

The U.S. government's disdainful reaction to Iraq's weapons of mass destruction programs rings hollow. American corporations have been supplying Iraq with components to build chemical and biological weapons for decades. And when Iraq used such weapons against Iran during the 1980s, the U.S. government was suspiciously silent because at that time Iran was considered a threat to U.S. interests in the Middle East. The United States only became vocal about Iraq's arsenal following Iraq's invasion of Kuwait in 1990 and the ensuing Gulf War. In light of American exports of chemicals and technology to Iraq, however, the U.S. government's outrage may backfire since some Gulf War veterans are claiming they were exposed to chemical weapons—weapons created with American aid—during the war.

The United States almost went to war against Iraq in February [1998] because of Saddam Hussein's weapons program. In his State of the Union address, President Clinton castigated Hussein for "developing nuclear, chemical, and biological weapons and the missiles to deliver them."

"You cannot defy the will of the world," the President proclaimed. "You have used weapons of mass destruction before. We are determined to deny you the capacity to use them again."

Most Americans listening to the President did not know that the United States supplied Iraq with much of the raw material for creating a chemical and biological warfare program. Nor did the media report that U.S. companies sold Iraq more than $1 billion worth of the components

Reprinted from "Anthrax for Export," by William Blum, *The Progressive*, April 1998, vol. 62, no. 4. Reprinted with permission.

needed to build nuclear weapons and diverse types of missiles, including the infamous Scud.

Selective involvement

When Iraq engaged in chemical and biological warfare in the 1980s, barely a peep of moral outrage could be heard from Washington, as it kept supplying Saddam with the materials he needed to build weapons. From 1980 to 1988, Iraq and Iran waged a terrible war against each other, a war that might not have begun if President Jimmy Carter had not given the Iraqis a green light to attack Iran, in response to repeated provocations. Throughout much of the war, the United States provided military aid and intelligence information to both sides, hoping that each would inflict severe damage on the other.

[Political and social theorist] Noam Chomsky suggests that this strategy is a way for America to keep control of its oil supply: "It's been a leading, driving doctrine of U.S. foreign policy since the 1940s that the vast and unparalleled energy resources of the Gulf region will be effectively dominated by the United States and its clients, and, crucially, that no independent indigenous force will be permitted to have a substantial influence on the administration of oil production and price."

When Iraq engaged in chemical and biological warfare in the 1980s, barely a peep of moral outrage could be heard from Washington, as it kept supplying Saddam with the materials he needed to build weapons.

During the Iran-Iraq war, Iraq received the lion's share of American support because at the time Iran was regarded as the greater threat to U.S. interests. According to a 1994 Senate report, private American suppliers, licensed by the U.S. Department of Commerce, exported a witch's brew of biological and chemical materials to Iraq from 1985 through 1989. Among the biological materials, which often produce slow, agonizing death, were:

- Bacillus Anthracis, cause of anthrax.
- Clostridium Botulinum, a source of botulinum toxin.
- Histoplasma Capsulatam, cause of a disease attacking lungs, brain, spinal cord, and heart.
- Brucella Melitensis, a bacteria that can damage major organs.
- Clostridium Perfringens, a highly toxic bacteria causing systemic illness.
- Clostridium tetani, a highly toxigenic substance.

Also on the list: Escherichia coli (E. coli), genetic materials, human and bacterial DNA, and dozens of other pathogenic biological agents. "These biological materials were not attenuated or weakened and were capable of reproduction," the Senate report stated. "It was later learned that these microorganisms exported by the United States were identical to those the United Nations inspectors found and removed from the Iraqi biological warfare program."

The report noted further that U.S. exports to Iraq included the precursors to chemical-warfare agents, plans for chemical and biological warfare production facilities, and chemical-warhead filling equipment. The exports continued to at least November 28, 1989, despite evidence that Iraq was engaging in chemical and biological warfare against Iranians and Kurds since as early as 1984.

Iraq's American suppliers

The American company that provided the most biological materials to Iraq in the 1980s was American Type Culture Collection of Maryland and Virginia, which made seventy shipments of the anthrax-causing germ and other pathogenic agents, according to a 1996 *Newsday* story.

Other American companies also provided Iraq with the chemical or biological compounds, or the facilities and equipment used to create the compounds for chemical and biological warfare. Among these suppliers were the following:

- Alcolac International, a Baltimore chemical manufacturer already linked to the illegal shipment of chemicals to Iran, shipped large quantities of thiodiglycol (used to make mustard gas) as well as other chemical and biological ingredients, according to a 1989 story in *The New York Times*.
- Nu Kraft Mercantile Corp. of Brooklyn (affiliated with the United Steel and Strip Corporation) also supplied Iraq with huge amounts of thiodiglycol, the *Times* reported.
- Celery Corp., Charlotte, NC
- Matrix-Churchill Corp., Cleveland, OH (regarded as a front for the Iraqi government, according to Representative Henry Gonzalez, Democrat of Texas, who quoted U.S. intelligence documents to this effect in a 1992 speech on the House floor).

The following companies were also named as chemical and biological materials suppliers in the 1992 Senate hearings on "United States export policy toward Iraq prior to Iraq's invasion of Kuwait":

- Mouse Master, Lilburn, GA
- Sullaire Corp., Charlotte, NC
- Pure Aire, Charlotte, NC
- Posi Seal, Inc., N. Stonington, CT
- Union Carbide, Danbury, CT
- Evapco, Taneytown, MD
- Gorman-Rupp, Mansfield, OH

Additionally, several other companies were sued in connection with their activities providing Iraq with chemical or biological supplies: subsidiaries or branches of Fisher Controls International, Inc., St. Louis; Rhone-Poulenc, Inc., Princeton, NJ; Bechtel Group, Inc., San Francisco; and Lummus Crest, Inc., Bloomfield, NJ, which built one chemical plant in Iraq and, before the Iraqi invasion of Kuwait in August 1990, was building an ethylene facility. Ethylene is a necessary ingredient for thiodiglycol.

In 1994, a group of twenty-six veterans, suffering from what has come to be known as Gulf War Syndrome, filed a billion-dollar lawsuit in

Houston against Fisher, Rhone-Poulenc, Bechtel Group, and Lummus Crest, as well as American Type Culture Collection (ATCC) and six other firms, for helping Iraq to obtain or produce the compounds which the veterans blamed for their illnesses. By 1998, the number of plaintiffs has risen to more than 4,000 and the suit is still pending in Texas.

[According to a Senate report] U.S. exports to Iraq included the precursors to chemical-warfare agents, plans for chemical and biological warfare production facilities, and chemical-warhead filling equipment.

A Pentagon study in 1994 dismissed links between chemical and biological weapons and Gulf War Syndrome. *Newsday* later disclosed, however, that the man who headed the study, Nobel laureate Joshua Lederberg, was a director of ATCC. Moreover, at the time of ATCC's shipments to Iraq, which the Commerce Department approved, the firm's CEO was a member of the Commerce Department's Technical Advisory Committee, the paper found.

A larger number of American firms supplied Iraq with the specialized computers, lasers, testing and analyzing equipment, and other instruments and hardware vital to the manufacture of nuclear weapons, missiles, and delivery systems. Computers, in particular, play a key role in nuclear weapons development. Advanced computers make it feasible to avoid carrying out nuclear test explosions, thus preserving the program's secrecy. The 1992 Senate hearings implicated the following firms:

- Kennametal, Latrobe, PA
- Hewlett Packard, Palo Alto, CA
- International Computer Systems, CA, SC, and TX
- Perkins-Elmer, Norwalk, CT
- BDM Corp., McLean, VA
- Leybold Vacuum Systems, Export, PA
- Spectra Physics, Mountain View, CA
- Unisys Corp., Blue Bell, PA
- Finnigan MAT, San Jose, Ca
- Scientific Atlanta, Atlanta, GA
- Spectral Data Corp., Champaign, IL
- Tektronix, Wilsonville, OR
- Veeco Instruments, Inc., Plainview, NY
- Wiltron Company, Morgan Hill, CA

The House report also singled out: TI Coating, Inc., Axel Electronics, Data General Corp., Gerber Systems, Honeywell, Inc., Digital Equipment Corp., Sackman Associates, Rockwell Collins International, Wild Magnavox Satellite Survey, Zeta Laboratories, Carl Schenck, EZ Logic Data, International Imaging Systems, Semetex Corp., and Thermo Jarrell Ash Corporation.

Some of the companies said later that they had no idea Iraq might ever put their products to military use. A spokesperson for Hewlett Packard said the company believed that the Iraqi recipient of its shipments, Saad 16, was an institution of higher learning. In fact, in 1990 *The*

Wall Street Journal described Saad 16 as "a heavily fortified, state-of-the-art complex for aircraft construction, missile design, and, almost certainly, nuclear-weapons research."

Other corporations recognized the military potential of their goods but considered it the government's job to worry about it. "Every once in a while you kind of wonder when you sell something to a certain country," said Robert Finney, president of Electronic Associates, Inc., which supplied Saad 16 with a powerful computer that could be used for missile testing and development. "But it's not up to us to make foreign policy," Finney told *The Wall Street Journal*.

U.S. government approves exports

In 1982, the Reagan Administration took Iraq off its list of countries alleged to sponsor terrorism, making it eligible to receive high-tech items generally denied to those on the list. Conventional military sales began in December of that year. Representative Samuel Gejdenson, Democrat of Connecticut, chairman of a House subcommittee investigating "United States Exports of Sensitive Technology to Iraq," stated in 1991:

"From 1985 to 1990, the United States Government approved 771 licenses for the export to Iraq of $1.5 billion worth of biological agents and high-tech equipment with military application. [Only thirty-nine applications were rejected.] The United States spent virtually an entire decade making sure that Saddam Hussein had almost whatever he wanted. . . . The Administration has never acknowledged that it took this course of action, nor has it explained why it did so. In reviewing documents and press accounts, and interviewing knowledgeable sources, it becomes clear that United States export-control policy was directed by U.S. foreign policy as formulated by the State Department, and it was U.S. foreign policy to assist the regime of Saddam Hussein."

From 1985 to 1990, the United States Government approved 771 licenses for the export to Iraq of $1.5 billion worth of biological agents and high-tech equipment with military application. . . . The United States spent virtually an entire decade making sure that Saddam Hussein had almost whatever he wanted.

Subsequently, Representative John Dingell, Democrat of Michigan, investigated the Department of Energy [DOE] concerning an unheeded 1989 warning about Iraq's nuclear weapons program. In 1992, he accused the DOE of punishing employees who raised the alarm and rewarding those who didn't take it seriously. One DOE scientist, interviewed by Dingell's Energy and Commerce Committee, was especially conscientious about the mission of the nuclear non-proliferation program. For his efforts, he received very little cooperation, inadequate staff, and was finally forced to quit in frustration. "It was impossible to do a good job," said William Emel. His immediate manager, who tried to get the proliferation program fully staffed, was chastened by management and removed from his position. Emel was hounded by the DOE at his new job as well.

Another Senate committee, investigating "United States export policy toward Iraq prior to Iraq's invasion of Kuwait," heard testimony in 1992 that Commerce Department personnel "changed information on sixty-eight licenses; that references to military end uses were deleted and the designation 'military truck' was changed. This was done on licenses having a total value of over $1 billion." Testimony made clear that the White House was "involved" in "a deliberate effort . . . to alter these documents and mislead the Congress."

American foreign-policy makers maintained a cooperative relationship with U.S. corporate interests in the region. In 1985, Marshall Wiley, former U.S. ambassador to Oman, set up the Washington-based U.S.-Iraq Business Forum, which lobbied in Washington on behalf of Iraq to promote U.S. trade with that country. Speaking of the Forum's creation, Wiley later explained, "I went to the State Department and told them what I was planning to do, and they said, 'Fine. It sounds like a good idea.' It was our policy to increase exports to Iraq."

Though the government readily approved most sales to Iraq, officials at Defense and Commerce clashed over some of them (with the State Department and the White House backing Commerce).

"If an item was in dispute, my attitude was if they were readily available from other markets, I didn't see why we should deprive American markets," explained Richard Murphy in 1990. Murphy was Assistant Secretary of State for Near Eastern and South Asian Affairs from 1983 to 1989.

One unexpected outcome

As it turned out, Iraq did not use any chemical or biological weapons against U.S. forces in the Gulf War. But American planes bombed chemical and biological weapons storage facilities with abandon, potentially dooming tens of thousands of American soldiers to lives of prolonged and permanent agony, and an unknown number of Iraqis to a similar fate. Among the symptoms reported by the affected soldiers are memory loss, scarred lungs, chronic fatigue, severe headache, raspy voice, and passing out. The Pentagon estimates that nearly 100,000 American soldiers were exposed to sarin gas alone.

After the war, White House and Defense Department officials tried their best to deny that Gulf War Syndrome had anything to do with the bombings. The suffering of soldiers was not their overriding concern. The top concerns of the Bush and Clinton Administrations were to protect perceived U.S. interests in the Middle East, and to ensure that American corporations still had healthy balance sheets.

Organizations to Contact

The editors have compiled the following list of organizations concerned with the issues debated in this book. The descriptions are derived from materials provided by the organizations. All have publications or information available for interested readers. The list was compiled on the date of publication of the present volume; names, addresses, phone and fax numbers, and e-mail addresses may change. Be aware that many organizations take several weeks or longer to respond to inquiries, so allow as much time as possible.

The American Civil Defense Association (TACDA)
PO Box 1057, Starke, FL 32091
(800) 425-5397 • (904) 964-5397 • fax: (904) 964-9641
e-mail: defense@tacda.org • website: www.tacda.org

TACDA was established in the early 1960s in an effort to help promote civil defense awareness and disaster preparedness, both in the military and private sector, and to assist citizens in their efforts to prepare for all types of natural and man-made disasters. Publications include the quarterly *Journal of Civil Defense* and the *TACDA Alert* newsletter.

Arms Control Association (ACA)
1726 M St. NW, Suite 201, Washington, DC 20036
(202) 463-8270 • fax: (202) 463-8273
e-mail: aca@armscontrol.org • website: www.armscontrol.org

The Arms Control Association is a nonprofit organization dedicated to promoting public understanding of and support for effective arms control policies. ACA seeks to increase public appreciation of the need to limit arms, reduce international tensions, and promote world peace. It publishes the monthly magazine *Arms Control Today*.

Center for Defense Information (CDI)
1779 Massachusetts Ave. NW, Suite 615, Washington, DC 20036
(202) 332-0600 • fax: (202) 462-4559
e-mail: info@cdi.org • website: www.cdi.org

CDI is comprised of civilians and former military officers who oppose both excessive expenditures for weapons and policies that increase the danger of war. The center serves as an independent monitor of the military, analyzing spending, policies, weapon systems, and related military issues. It publishes the *Defense Monitor* ten times per year.

Center for Nonproliferation Studies
Monterey Institute of International Studies
425 Van Buren St., Monterey, CA 93940
(831) 647-4154 • fax: (831) 647-3519
website: http://cns.miis.edu

The center researches all aspects of nonproliferation and works to combat the spread of weapons of mass destruction. The center produces research databases and has multiple reports, papers, speeches, and congressional testimony available online. Its main publication is *The Nonproliferation Review*, which is published three times per year.

Chemical and Biological Arms Control Institute
2111 Eisenhower Ave., Suite 302, Alexandria, VA 22314
(703) 739-1538 • fax: (703) 739-1525
e-mail: cbaci@cbaci.org • website: www.cbaci.org

The institute is a nonprofit corporation that supports arms control and nonproliferation, particularly of chemical and biological weapons. In addition to conducting research, the institute plans meetings and seminars and assists in the implementation of weapons-control treaties. Its publications include *The Dispatch*, published bimonthly, and numerous fact sheets, monographs, and reports.

Henry L. Stimson Center
11 Dupont Circle NW, 9th Floor, Washington, DC 20036
(202) 223-5956 • fax: (202) 238-9604
website: www.stimson.org

The Stimson Center is an independent, nonprofit public policy institute committed to finding and promoting innovative solutions to the security challenges confronting the United States and other nations. The center directs the Chemical and Biological Weapons Nonproliferation Project, which serves as a clearinghouse of information related to the monitoring and implementation of the 1993 Chemical Weapons Convention. The center produces occasional papers, reports, handbooks, and books on chemical and biological weapon policy, nuclear policy, and eliminating weapons of mass destruction.

Peace Action
1819 H St. NW, Suite 420, Washington, DC 20006
(202) 862-9740 • fax: (202) 862-9762
e-mail: paprog@igc.org • website: www.peace-action.org

Peace Action is a grassroots peace and justice organization that works for policy changes in Congress and the United Nations, as well as state and city legislatures. The national office houses an Organizing Department that promotes education and activism on topics related to peace and disarmament issues. The organization produces a quarterly newsletter and also publishes an annual voting record for members of Congress.

United States Arms Control and Disarmament Agency (ACDA)
320 21st St. NW, Washington, DC 20451
(800) 581-ACDA • fax: (202) 647-6928
website: www.acda.gov

The mission of the agency is to strengthen the national security of the United States by formulating, advocating, negotiating, implementing, and verifying effective arms control, nonproliferation, and disarmament policies, strategies, and agreements. In so doing, ACDA ensures that arms control is fully integrated into the development and conduct of U.S. national security policy. The agency publishes fact sheets on the disarmament of weapons of mass destruction as well as online records of speeches, treaties, and reports related to arms control.

Bibliography

Books

Ken Alibek with
Stephen Handelman
Biohazard: The Chilling True Story of the Largest Covert Biological Weapons Program in the World—Told from the Inside by the Man Who Ran It. New York: Random House, 1999.

Leonard A. Cole
The Eleventh Plague: The Politics of Biological and Chemical Warfare. New York: W.H. Freeman, 1996.

Hugh D. Crone
Banning Chemical Weapons: The Scientific Background. New York: Cambridge University Press, 1992.

Richard A. Falkenrath, Robert D. Newman, and Bradley A. Thayer
America's Achilles' Heel: Nuclear, Biological, and Chemical Terrorism and Covert Attack. Cambridge, MA: MIT Press, 1998.

Avigdor Haselkorn
The Continuing Storm: Iraq, Poisonous Weapons, and Deterrence. New Haven, CT: Yale University Press, 1999.

Stuart E. Johnson, ed.
The Niche Threat: Deterring the Use of Chemical and Biological Weapons. Washington, DC: National Defense University, 1997.

Joshua Lederberg, ed.
Biological Weapons: Limiting the Threat (BCSIA Studies in International Security), Cambridge, MA: MIT Press, 1999.

Tom Mangold and
Jeff Goldberg
Plague Wars: A True Story of Biological Warfare. New York: St. Martin's, 2000.

Richard M. Price
The Chemical Weapons Taboo. Ithaca, NY: Cornell University Press, 1997.

Edward Regis
The Biology of Doom: The History of America's Secret Germ Warfare Project. New York: Henry Holt, 1999.

Tim Trevan
Saddam's Secrets: The Hunt for Iraq's Hidden Weapons. North Pomfret, VT: Trafalgar Square, 1999.

Stansfield Turner
Caging the Genies: A Workable Solution for Nuclear, Chemical, and Biological Weapons. Boulder, CO: Westview, 1999.

Raymond A. Zilinskas, ed.
Biological Warfare: Modern Offense and Defense. Boulder, CO: Lynne Rienner, 1999.

Periodicals

Philip H. Abelson
"Biological Warfare," *Science*, November 26, 1999.

CQ Researcher
"Chemical and Biological Weapons," January 31, 1997. Available from 1414 22nd St. NW, Washington, DC 20037.

Economist   "Coming Soon to a City Near You," August 15, 1998.

T. Trent Gegax and   "The New Bomb Threat," *Newsweek*, March 22, 1999.
Mark Hosenball

Thomas Graham Jr.   "Time for a No-First-Use Policy," *The Christian Science
and Elizabeth   Monitor*, January 28, 1999.
R. Rindskopf

Christopher Hitchens   "Outrage: Displaced and Misplaced," *Nation*, December
                           13, 1999.

David E. Kaplan   "The Chem-Bio Attacks That Never Were," *U.S. News &
                           World Report*, October 18, 1999.

Diego Lluma   "Low Probability, High Consequence," *Bulletin of the
                           Atomic Scientists*, November/December 1999.

Richard Lugar and   "An End to Chemical Weapons," *Christian Science
Joseph Biden   Monitor*, February 28, 1997.

Judith Miller   "U.S. Aid Is Diverted to Germ Warfare, Russian Scientists
                           Say," *New York Times*, January 25, 2000.

Judith Miller   "U.S. Helps Russia Turn Germ Center to Peace Uses,"
                           New York Times, January 8, 2000.

Chitra Ragavan and   "The Boom in Bioterror Funds," *U.S. News & World
David E. Kaplan   Report*, October 18, 1999.

Scott D. Sagan   "The Commitment Trap: Why the United States Should
                           Not Use Nuclear Threats to Deter Biological and Chemi-
                           cal Weapons Attacks," *International Security*, Spring 2000.

Calvin Sims   "Koreans See Dark Scenario in a U.S. Precaution," *New
                           York Times*, December 26, 1999.

John F. Sopko   "The Changing Proliferation Threat," *Foreign Policy*,
                           December 1, 1996.

Jose Vegar   "Terrorism's New Breed," *Bulletin of the Atomic Scientists*,
                           March/April 1998.

Evelyn L. Wright   "Taking Aim at the Nightmare Bug," *Business Week*,
                           November 1, 1999.

Index